BLOCK HOUSING

BLOCK HOUSING

A CONTEMPORARY PERSPECTIVE

PERE JOAN RAVETLLAT MIRA

GG

Editorial Gustavo Gili, S.A.

08029 Barcelona   Rosselló, 87-89
Spain
Tel. (343) 322 81 61   Fax (343) 322 92 05

Translation: Graham Thomson
Cover design: Eulàlia Coma

© Editorial Gustavo Gili, S.A., Barcelona, 1992

ISBN: 84-252-1567-6
Depósito legal: B. 18.830-1992
Printed in Spain by Grafos, S. A. Arte sobre papel

Contents

The origins of a type.
A contemporary perspective

Words often reach a point where they lose their original meaning or become drained of content. Indiscriminate usage, excessive misuse or the universal acceptance of only one of their senses frequently blurs their outlines. This may well be the explanation behind the fact that the term 'apartment block' is currently used to refer to almost any residential building, having by now become separated from its originally accepted sense in the 1920s. Although awareness of and concern with the problem of housing both pre-and post-dates that period, the intentions set out in those early prototypes give them a social dimension, affirmative and charged with hope, which it is no easy matter to recover now.

The industrial city and the resulting increase in population density is an unavoidable reference and starting point for many of the ways in which the theme of housing has been approached in this century. The communal environments proposed by Robert Owen, or Charles Fourier's Falansterie, are alternative visions from the the first half of the 19th century, directed towards dissolving the incipient dualism between city and country at the same time as they called for a more balanced, juster society. The communal settlements described by Fournier proposed a return to the solemnity represented by Versailles, in an attempt to restore dignity to an architecture impoverished by the propagation of small houses which proliferated on the outskirts of the urban centres. Rejected by the scientific socialists (Marx, Engels) as well as by a bourgeoisie inspired by the restructuring of its cities, which was to consolidate the model of the 19th century familiar to us now, the few such settlements actually established (New Lanark, 1815, and Guisa, 1859-70) represented so many failures to reorient the new industrial world in the direction of a structure based on small communities.

The garden city models which appeared at the end of the century mark a step forward at the same time as they manifest a dissatisfaction with the quality of life in the cities, asserting an urban scale more in tune with the individual. Rail transport was to be the key to defining both the axial layout put forward by A. Soria y Mata, who only managed to partially construct his project for Madrid, and the concentric scheme proposed by E. Howard, which was subsequently adopted in the building of the English new towns.

As early as the first part of the 20th century, the proposals for certain districts of Rotterdam (Spangen or Tusschendijken) projected by M. Brinkman and J. J. P. Oud, alongside the prototype Domino house formulated by Le Corbusier in 1915 and the development of the new technologies of iron, glass and reinforced concrete presaged and to some extent ushered in the significant proposal for the 'Immeuble-Villa' made by Le Corbusier in 1922. This proposal, designed for very high-density occupation, was constructed on the basis of juxtaposed duplex cells which included individual garden-terraces. These units were built up to a height of six units, leaving a rectangular space in the centre for the laying out of accesses and recreational amenities for the community. Halfway between the socialist housing collective and the traditional apartment building –the very name 'Immeuble-Villa' reflects this dichotomy–, the sheer size of the floor areas envisaged (370 m2 for the typical unit) and the double-height terraces and living rooms made their widespread adoption enormously difficult. The Pavilion de l'Esprit Nouveau was the only material expression of the idea, presented at the Paris Exhibition in 1925 in an attempt at promoting the cell as a self-sufficient unit independent of the complex as a whole.

After the 'Immeuble-Villa', the Twenties were marked by the effort to define, delimit and interrelate the parameters into which the function of living could rationally be divided. From A. Klein's studies in the combination of elements for the interior of the dwelling to W. Gropius' calculations directed towards establishing the optimum proportions of height and separation between blocks, every quantifiable feature was minutely analysed. With the distribution being rationalised to do away with superfluous internal passages, or the groupings of service nuclei conceived as authentic machine rooms, the whole came together in radical new visions of urban design.

In this context, special mention must be made of L. Hilberseimer's vertical city, in which the uses are superimposed on one another vertically. Housing, culture, offices, all grouped together in the same building, take the place of the traditional homogeneous accumulation of activities. As in the mediaeval city, the laying out of the residential city on top of the commercial city or the work city was to result in a reduction in traffic, since only vertical movement would be necessary, with no need to go out into the exterior. This would, evidently, lead to the disappearance of absurd and lengthy journeys and the chaos of construction brought about by the individual private house.

Even so, the challenge of building still remained: the perfection of methods, the reduction of costs and the coherent utilisation of the new materials were the objectives which illustrated the text of Hannes Meyer's 'Construction' (1928).

"... Everything in the world is the product of a formula [function x economics].

Familisterio de Guisa. Aerial view.
Familisterio de Guisa. View of the roofed internal courtyard in its present state.
Aerial view of Letchworth.

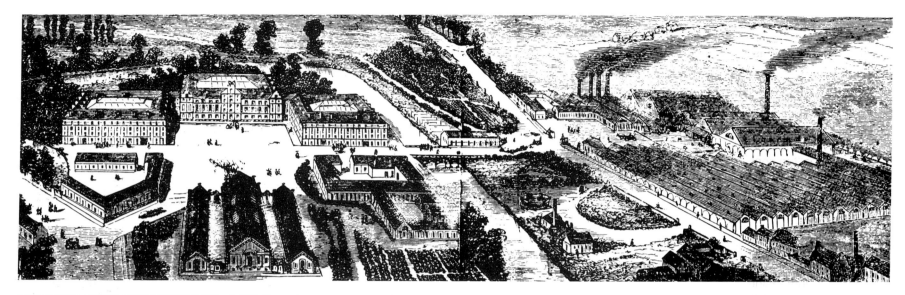

General view of Spangen,
Rotterdam. M. Brinkman and J.J.P.
Oud, 1919-1920.
Axonometric drawing of Spangen,
Rotterdam. M. Brinkman and J.J.P.
Oud, 1919-1920.

Thus, none of these things is a work of art.
All art is composition, and is therefore not adapted to a particular end.
All life is function and as such is not artistic.
The idea of composing a port is simply comical.
But how to design the plan of a city, or a dwelling?
Composition or function? Art or life?
Construction is a biological process. Construction is not an aesthetic process.
Architecture as 'the emotional act of the artist' is without justification.
Architecture as 'the continuation of the constructive tradition' means letting oneself be carried along by History. ..."

The residential district of Torten, in Germany, –constructed by W. Gropius in 1926-28– exemplifies some of the content of Meyer's text, and constituted a major contribution to the endeavour to standardise and rationalise construction methods. A linear process of fabrication and assembly allowed workers to be assigned to a single stage in the process, thus increasing their productivity. The use of a system of mobile cranes running on rails serving every part of the site facilitated the positioning of beams and panels manufactured in situ, contributing further to the increase in productive capacity.

Parallel to this, the formation of the O.S.A. group (Association of Contemporary Architects) in the Soviet Union, under the direction of M. Ginzburg, saw the group adopt as one of its primary objectives the study of prototypes for the dom-kommuna communal apartment building. By means of the competition organised by the group's review, S.A. (Contemporary Architecture), on the theme of collective housing, the group arrived at a definition of the Strojkom cell. The result was a set of five alternative typologies, and the whole experience crystallised in the Narkomfin building (Moscow, 1929). A building for 1100 occupants designed by Ginzburg and Miljutin, the entrance bears an inscription announcing, 'The members of the communal house are more obliged than others to take part in the struggle for collective organisation'.

Many of these endeavours were debated and contrasted at the congresses in Frankfurt in 1929 and Brussels in 1930, the former taking the title of Existenzminimum, and the latter having the aim of forging ahead with the definition of rational construction methods. No doubt the fact that the congress was held in Frankfurt, an immense display cabinet filled with numerous constructions by Ernst May, determined the direction of debate around the already sufficiently oppressive concept of minimal habitability. From his first project in Bruchfeldstrasse in 1926, in which a scheme of modules with a

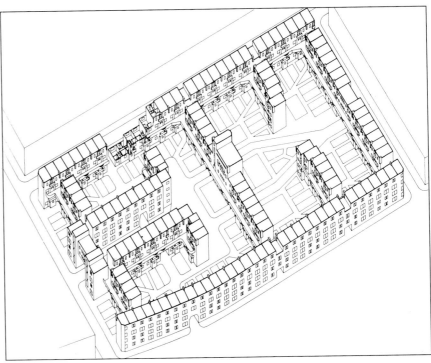

stepped plan delimited a carefully ordered interior space, E. May had painstakingly developed his ideas which, following the guidelines of the Neue Frankfurt urban plan, culminated in his work on the districts of Praunheim and Rommerstadt. In these latter projects, a strict criterion of surface area, together with a pioneering system of lightweight prefabricated partitions (the May system), and the notable incorporation of the 'Frankfurt kitchen' allowed him to construct more than 15,000 homes in the space of only a few years.

Le Corbusier's rhetoric could not easily accept these rigid Germanic formulations, and, more concerned with developing a representative prototype for the new machine age than with following a line that was not sufficiently representative of the mood of the time, his subsequent evolution was in marked contrast to the line laid down at the congress. At all events, and in spite of his disagreement with the concerns expressed in Frankfurt, his proposal for the Ville Radieuse was in tune with some points of that programme, putting its faith in concepts radically opposed to those of the 'Immeuble-Villa' project. In this new approach to the question, the landscaped terraces and double-height spaces make way for apartments economically laid out over one level. The exuberant scale and the single programme have evolved towards a solution that is flexible, adaptable, and capable of transformation by means of sliding room-dividers. Industrialised construction methods and strict economic viability underlie a prototype designed for eventual incorporation in the decentralised city free of any kind of hierarchy, where a layout in the form of parallel strips allows for infinite extension.

The aim of this rapid overview of the parameters which defined the *raison d'etre* of the apartment building in the nineteen-twenties is to provide a basic frame of reference for some of the numerous and complex developments undergone by the concepts described below.

Taking as its starting point considerations of the importance of the typological scheme, the idea of the city associated with the proposals, systems of construction and thematic aspects of the residential programme, these concepts are analysed in terms of the projects presented here. Rather than being an exercise in classification, this is in effect a more fragmentary approach, using the concepts mentioned above as a means of arriving at a clearer understanding of the idea of the apartment building.

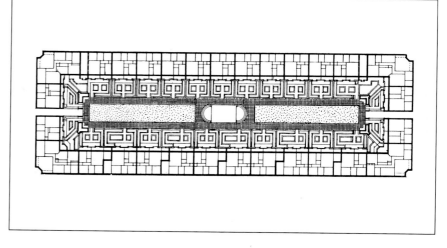

Immeuble-Villas. General plan,
perspective and view of the exterior.
Le Corbusier, 1922.

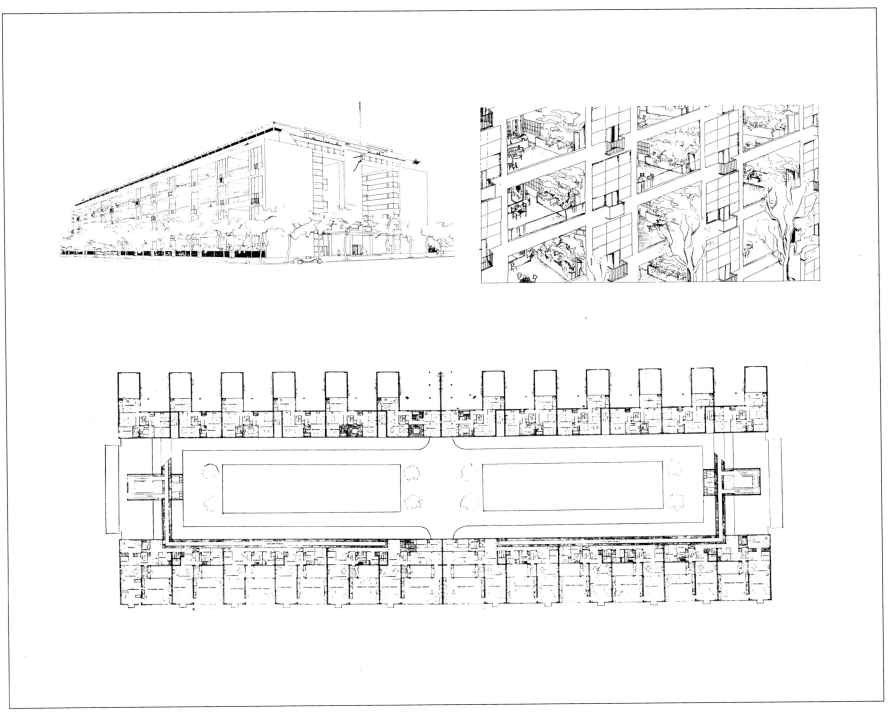

The linear model as circulation-type

It would be hard to find a constant of greater value in explaining the nature of the block than that of the predominant role of its linear dimension. The prototype, conceived as the juxtaposition of a series of elements, thus explicitly reveals its rejection of limits and the mechanisms which make this possible.

Circulation elements are intrinsically involved in this linearity, and both their situation and the spatial characteristics of the areas they configure make them one of the clearest features of this type of compositional group. Their very characteristics make them susceptible to clear systematisation, and thus readily analysable down to their ultimate consequences, so that, right from the outset, they invite classification and comparison between the various alternative options. At the same time, their form and layout directly influence the type, here the binomial relationship of circulation-type, which encourages the notion of the block as a series of pieces which together constitute a perfect machine.

As an instance of this, the building by D. and R. Thut in Erding, a small town to the north-west of Munich, specifically invests value in its three entrances, relating them to the urban grid in the midst of which the building stands, in a residential district on the edge of the town centre. The construction is laid out on the basis of these different passageways on the ground floor, going from the most centrally situated, with its spiral staircase, to the small access at the far end of the building, leaving the gently sloping ramp between them as a one-off element. In this way, the three different types of accessibility interpret their own specific relationships with the project, adapting in each case to meet particular needs.

The importance of these aspects is even more apparent in A. Siza's project for The Hague, in which it would be difficult to analyse their configuration without pausing to note the delicate reinterpretation of a traditional system of accessibility which entirely determines the resolution of the floor plan. The successive flights of stairs give private access to every floor and thus manage to preserve the same distribution scheme at the same time as they compose the double-height entrance space.

The building in Dockhaven harbour in Rotterdam by D.K.V. and J. Nouvel's Nemausus I in Nîmes each exemplifies, from a different standpoint, the same clear intention of rendering its linear potential explicit. The concern with the rational definition of the floor plan, conceived as an indefinitely extensible series of cells, and the

circulation system both generate this notion of the linear model based on the same potentially unlimited extension of one dimension. The expression of this schematic potentiality, or a frequently optimising approach, have often prompted references to the mythology of the machine, in a clear allusion to the world of engineering.

In the case of Rotterdam, the linearity of the scheme reinforces its strategic emplacement overlooking the Niewe-Maas river, and its considerable height of eleven storeys allows it to enjoy exceptionally fine views. The duplex apartments, each with its own gallery, are framed by the twin entrances, connecting them with the neighbouring building and the remarkable curved space in the form of a ship's prow which relates the circulation spaces by means of a splendid vista of their surroundings. Both facades reveal their internal configuration, defined by the horizontal banding which emphasizes their length.

In Nîmes, J. Nouvel's scheme proposes a versatile programme on one, two or three levels, offering a total of seventeen different possible types, all set at right angles to the line of the block, thus giving them views from both facades. Access is in every case by way of the communal corridors, with their lightweight balustrades of perforated sheet metal, which continue on into the porches of the apartments. The industrial finishes, the treatment of the roof, the transparency of the ground floors, and the special beacons for nighttime illumination clearly demonstrate a consciously sought-after engineering aesthetic.

There are, however, schemes which use a similar organisational grouping to give the project a less dominant character. 'The Imperial', in Miami, one of the most obvious a priori examples of the linear block, abandons the expression of mechanistic typologies to concentrate on scenic possibilities. The populist reduction of the principles of the Modern Movement is transformed here into an expressive collage whose vivid colours and pure geometries seem to spontaneously generate themselves. The architecture, which here becomes the built image of a particular culture, takes as its principles the promotion of the building as symbol and the superimposition of monumental elements onto the block, which serves as backdrop. With 'The Imperial', Arquitectonica have constructed the evident metaphor of a great window opening onto the bay, in harmony with the cultural tradition of the great North American building.

D. Liebeskind's scheme developed along Flottwellstrasse in Berlin employs further allegorical aspects of the block, stripping it of its more conventional attributes. The 450 metre-long building rises up at a slightly oblique six degree angle to make way for passage beneath it.

Organised around a central passageway which gradually evolves from a historic boulevard into the avenue which marks out the urban structure of the future city, the photographs of the model reveal the building from every angle and in all its aspects. This model is constructed of scraps of paper from architects' drawings, telephone directories, maps, bibles, banknotes ..., anything which can be readily cut up and used in fashioning the volume.

The implicit city

At the start of this analysis we looked at how, in the years from 1920 to 1930, the typology of the proposed construction was substantially bound up with the whole idea of the city, with this link in turn effectively constituting one of the factors in the profoundly innovative spirit of the period. If the application of rationalist criteria to the grouping together of cells on the basis of the circulation scheme determined the so-called linear model, the juxtaposition of buildings designed in terms of this model sought to transform the traditional nineteenth century conception of the city. From Le Corbusier's Ville Radieuse to L. Hilberseimer's vertical city, from W. Gropius' studies for the siting of the city dwelling to E. May's urban design work in Frankfurt, the residential schemes of those years were indissolubly linked to radical perspectives for the renovation of the city, in both morphology and infrastructure.

It is highly instructive to note, in spite of the great distance which separates us now from those ambitious aims, the relationship established with the context in many of the projects presented here.

Adaptation to the urban grid thus emerges as one of the most common factors relating the building to its setting on the basis of changes in typology.

The portion of a city block designed by Diener and Diener in Basle is effectively generated by its specific approximation to its context. Standing in an industrial area of the city, the scheme is divided into three facades, each looking onto a different street, and each imbued with a particular character which brings it into relation with its surroundings. The fact that each of the blocks incorporates different types of public and private use adds an experimental approach to the urban space and its connection with the housing to the contradictions inherent in the site itself. The scheme's maintenance of the unity of the whole without lessening the singular character of each one of its parts,

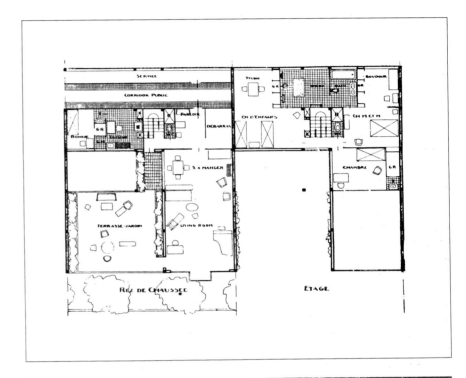

Scheme for a city of skyscrapers, north-south street. View of the vertical city. Ludwig Hilberseimer. Pavilion de l'Esprit Nouveau at the International Exhibition of Decorative Arts. View of the dining room. Le Corbusier, 1925.

each linked exclusively to a particular environment, is its greatest achievement.

Interrelation with the urban fabric also plays an essentially definitive role in the project by E. Bonell in Sabadell, in which the circular configuration is of the plaza and the considerable buildable depth are determining factors. The repetition of a single module based on adaptation to the geometry of the perimeter simultaneously resolves both siting and volume, with a great economy of means. Through the use of rectilinear planes, the groups of two apartments to a stairwell adapt to the contours of the space while ensuring that the majority of the living areas are orthogonal. In the interior, the living room-dining room areas take on the key role in resolving the agreement of the different geometries, since their location allows them to define the composition of the whole. Seen from the rear, the smooth regular convexity of the complex is modulated by the bands of openings lighting the service cores, while the stairs at either end of the building resolve its union with the existing urban fabric.

The complexity of introducing a new structure into certain urban environments is reflected in H. Kollhoff's scheme for an area adjoining the Charlottenburg castle. Three blocks, similar in height to their neighbours, emerge from the midst of the classical buildings which have managed to survive until the present in the city of Berlin. The curving wall which defines the scheme continues the line established by Schinkel's pavilion, built in 1824, with regard to the orthogonal relationship with the street-axes. The cross-shaped plan of the second block orders the composition of its volumes opposite the Schloss Garten. The compactness of the three volumes is maintained by the transparent curtain wall and the potent gable-end of the roof, constituting an impressive urban image which takes its place in, at the same time as it redefines, its setting.

The relationship with the existing urban fabric also serves as the basis for J. Ll. Mateo's scheme in Poble Nou, Barcelona, which manifests the tensions set up by the existing buildings and the regular grid of the Cerdà Eixample on which it was to be superimposed. The cumulative rhythm created by the repetition of an elementary residential unit is interrupted by the walls, which respond in different ways to the specific context of their situation. While the wall of fair-faced brick is interrupted on the Cerdà corner to be formally defined as an excavated solid which reveals the geometric complexity of this point, the Pallars corner emphasises the existing alignment by means of the regular window sequence, with its evident desire for integration.

Other interventions, such as the J. Herzog & P. de Meuron scheme in Schwarz Park, Basle, have their origins in acute reflections on place and form; neither determining them from the exterior nor defining them in advance. In the Schwarz Park project, the internal structure of the building determines the section, the floor plans and the facades, expressing its potent geometry in its relationship with the imposing volume of the neighbouring Bethesda hospital, which also stands on a plateau bounded by a water meadow by the edge of the river. A compact housing module provides the unit of repetition, and as it advances longitudinally the block composes its dimensions at the same time as it changes its materials. Much of the interest of this project stems from the manner in which, by means of this cumulative approach, attached yet public spaces are defined, generated by large-scale elements of flat planes and geometries, identical yet displaced, twisting round through the full extent of their vertical development. Considered in this way, the building can be compared to some conglomerate material in which each of the components retains its own individual character in the final appearance.

The absence of clearly defined axes in a peripheral zone adjoining a major traffic intersection characterises the setting for F. J. Sáenz de Oiza's remarkable intervention in Madrid. A plot with no effective context, an island amidst the surrounding roads, has given rise to an introspective scheme which close in on itself for protection from the exterior. The block curves in a spiral with its point of origin at the geometrical centre, climbing upwards as it responds to different urban circumstances. The facade which gives onto the M-30 expressway, of red brick, is divided up by its rows of little windows, while the interior, radically different, is painted, with a surprising colourist sequence which follows the rhythm of the paired terraces of the duplex apartments.

As a final observation in this section, I feel that mention must be made of the reflections on the city made manifest by A. Kitagawara in his 'Cloudy-Spoon' project for the Hoya district of Tokyo. For this Japanese architect, the real vision of the city is not to be found in a book, through a window or on a stroll, but in the electronic images emitted by television screens or in films. The city runs in disorder towards mechanisms of self-expression which reveal it as an excessive combination of living ruins which make up a labyrinth. His architecture has no grander objective than to constitute a fragment of the metropolis, an accumulation of interior cities in need of time in order to form itself as a space.

Structure, Construction, Materials

The typology expressed in the linear model and the city implicit in the residential proposal were both characterised to an equal degree by the rationalism at work in their structural and constructive definition. Attempts at prefabrication, the introduction of new technologies, and the recognition of the importance of materials, in terms of their utilisation as much as their signification, all contributed to the idea of the block and its distancing from the construction methods employed in the past. Once again the connection between system of construction, typology and city reinforced the concept of the universal prototype put forward as a general solution to all the aspects involved in housing design.

The Finnish architects E. Kairamo, K. Gullichsen and T. Vormala make disciplined use of the elements which constitute the modern tradition in their country. Operating within a cultural context historically receptive to the formal and technical innovations of the twenties and thirties, this team of architects reworks a modern vocabulary which culminates in a logical expression showing considerable sensitivity in the way in which it relates to the surrounding landscape. As in the majority of buildings of recent design in the same area, here a system of construction based on precast concrete elements framed by steel strips on the exterior has been used. The precast panels, clad with ceramic tiles, articulate the facades modelled by the groups of in situ concrete balconies.

In marked contrast to the modulated discretion of the previous project, S. Takamatsu opts, in his 'Cube III' scheme, for an emphatic expressiveness in the structural elements of which it is composed. The facade is divided into two: a socle which serves to reinforce the base of the building, consisting of a regular grid of columns, and, above this, the cross-like arrangement which groups together the apartments of the top two floors. The delicate hierarchy presented by the sequence of transparent and opaque outer skins of the balconies in terms of scale generates a detached facade for the apartment block and its roof, with its concrete cylinders vertically individualising each of the different apartments.

The use of industrial materials combines the laudable aim of keeping down costs with a reference to technology and mass production. The exhaustive effort which went into Nemausus I, mentioned above, is exemplary in this context. The industrial nature of each and every one of the materials used made for an extremely uncomplicated construction process and the minimum of subsequent maintenance.

Törten, Dessau. General floor plan. Walter Gropius, 1926-1928.
Scheme for a city of skyscrapers, east-west street. View of the vertical city. Ludwig Hilberseimer.

Törten, Dessau. Consumers' cooperative building. Walter Gropius, 1926-1928.

Project for a city. Ludwig Hilberseimer.
Törten, Dessau. Terraced houses forming a square. Walter Gropius, 1926-1928.

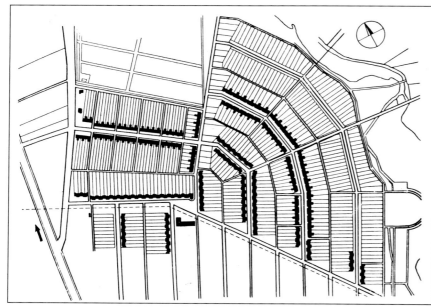

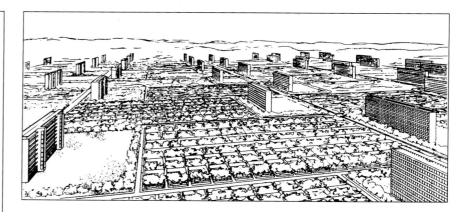

Törten, Dessau. Site plan for a
group of houses laid out along
tracks for cranes. Walter Gropius.

Thus, the doors on the terraces which make it possible to open up the
entire facade to the exterior space are the same as those used in car
parks for large vehicles; the metal stairs are those used in the steel
industry; the industrial flooring is of the continuous type to be found in
airports or department stores and the PVC sunshades are widely used
in agriculture. The choice of materials, all selected from catalogues, is
a manifesto in itself, in favour of the industrial contribution to residential
architecture.

In parallel with this, N. Grimshaw's scheme for Grand Union Walk,
London, largely consists in the application of sophisticated
technologies to a problematic site. The distribution of the dwellings is
derived from the impediments created by their position, especially as
regards the provision of daylight in the interiors of those apartments
with no direct south-facing openings. The L-shaped plan allows the
bedroom in the double space to look onto the large glass door-cum-
window, with its industrial vertical-opening system. This automatic
mechanism means that the double-height corridor is able to act as an
exterior space when the large glass door giving onto the canal is swung
back in the summer months. The privacy of the interior of the
apartments is ensured by the electrically-operated aluminium slats
positioned on the exterior, which can be moved up and down
independently of the doors they screen. Facades and roofs, also
formed of aluminium panels, put the finishing touches to the clearly
technological character of Grimshaw's scheme.

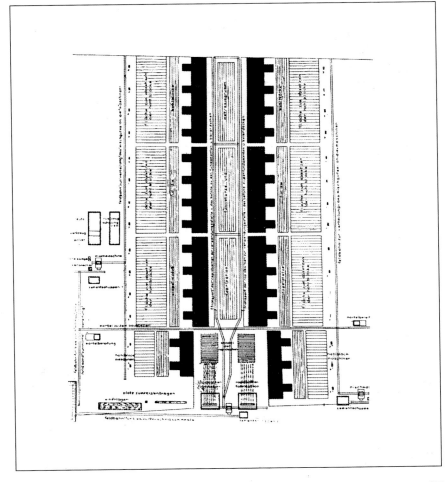

The alternative programme

The desire to improve the residents' ways of living, rationalise the housing programme and provide the community with all the facilities needed for individuals to fulfil themselves constitute the last of the four component aspects with which we have set out to define the fundamental values of the apartment block.

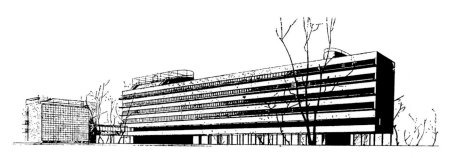

The ideas of flexibility of use, rationalisation of internal circulation and the orderly laying out of the different living areas have also converted the definition of the programme into a proposal for an alternative lifestyle, an alternative way of living. Alongside this, the idea of community, still imbued with something of Fourier's thesis, has contributed to the development of the capacity for self-sufficiency in housing complexes, equipping them with essential communal services.

The Coop-Himmelblau architects' cooperative formulated the basic rights of the resident in their scheme for Vienna: the right to live in a spatious, economic environment in which the individual was free to intervene as and when he or she chose. The designers defined their complex as 'open architecture', free, unencumbered with false significations. The project consists of two oblique volumes whose displacement produces inclined surfaces, with two bodies in the form of a flame emerging from between them: these contain fifty apartments whose tenants themselves are left free to decide on the finish of the interiors. Each apartment is different in its measurements, surface area and distribution, although all are laid out over two levels. There is also an additional built space of some thousand square metres for the free use of the residents.

Equally revealing is the relationship with the brief established in the 'Hybrid Building' by S. Holl, conceived for a 'society of strangers'. '...The building is divided in its upper levels into two volumes differentiated by their orientation. The west-facing block, receiving light from the setting sun, with its facade looking onto the central square, is intended for sociable types who get up late and like action through to the small hours. All of the apartments have two levels, are identical, and fitted with luxury bathrooms, microwaves and party areas.

The east-looking apartments, oriented towards the rising sun and the dawn, are intended for melancholy individuals. These like to wake early, to enjoy silence and solitude. The melancholy types for whom these dwellings were conceived are: a tragic poet, a musician and a mathematician. For this reason the floor plans and sections of the three apartment types are developed along the same lines.'

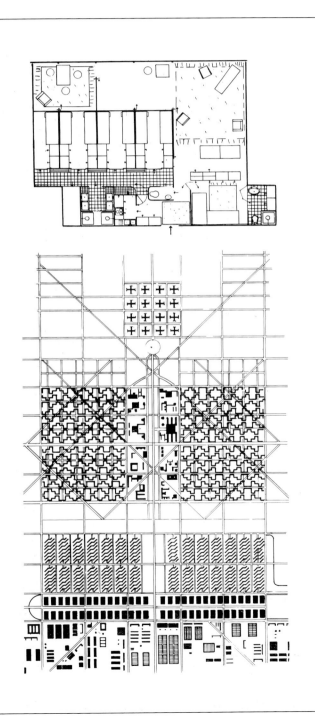

A fascinating example of how, starting from an anecdotal brief such as that of constructing a housing complex facing onto a square, it is possible to evolve an imaginative and individualised architectonic conception according to the premises of its occupants.

Of great interest, too, is the experience constituted by D. and R. Thut's scheme in Erding, referred to earlier in this introduction, in which the future residents were involved in the actual construction of the block. Their participation principally took the form of work on the interior finishing of the apartments, where they had the opportunity to convert the open-air balconies and terraces into enclosed glazed galleries, thus obtaining additional living space. The evident intention of adapting the programme is reflected in the differentiated distribution schemes of the apartments, which respond to different ways of living and using the space. Two laundries, a site set aside for washing cars and a sun-terrace, together with various other facilities, indicate a clear desire for independence and self-sufficiency.

Architects: Alvaro Siza Vieira, Carlos Castanheira

Collaborators: Fred van den Burg, Liesbeth Alfenrink

Ponto e Vírgula

Schilderswijk-Centrum
Zone 5

1984-1991   The Hague (NL)

Zone 5 constitutes a portion of the land belonging to the Urban Renovation Plan for Schilderwijk Centrum. This plan was developed by Siza on the basis of studies of the existing urban structure, with its large-scale apartment buildings housing workers and their families, constructed according to the planning norms of 1906 and now showing serious problems in their foundations, making the demolition of certain sectors unavoidable, even in cases of considerable architectural quality.

The residents - some 50 % of whom are immigrants- are organised into neighbourhood associations, each with its own community centre, which has helped ensure an active dialogue with the city authorities responsible for the first studies. The conflict between the desire to conserve the image which the city has evolved through the course of its history and a desire for change has resulted in the conclusion that the optimum solution is to construct a dense, complex scheme which makes no alteration to the existing urban fabric.

To achieve this, priority was given to issues concerning the character of the street, accessibility and safety in the overlaying of pedestrian and vehicular traffic, the use and maintenance of the public spaces, and the internal organisation of the apartments. These premises took concrete form in the design of long streets defined by continuous facades which completely enclosed the blocks, characterised by the regular rhythm of the openings, emphasising the corners in order to clearly define public and private spaces. At the same time, the apartments are grouped in four-storey blocks, thus making for a uniformity in the use of typologies without sacrificing the project's capacity to respond to the cultural variety and specific requirements of the residents. Wherever possible, the apartments have direct independent access in the form of a portico, while access to the garages has been unified as a single entrance giving onto the street. In the typology of the portico, which had been completely neglected for years, the Portuguese architect found the form which satisfied the wishes and needs expressed by the community's representatives as well as resolving a series of safety problems which affect the area;

although the portico is normally used to provide access to three floors, here it has been transformed to allow direct access to the fourth.

The solution adopted in the interior of the apartments is functional and flexible, in that its sliding doors make it possible to vary the degree of privacy in the relationships between different rooms, thus facilitating the adaptation of these dwellings to the needs of the different racial groups living in the neighbourhood.

The evolution of the Plan has been geared to a basic programme, to be followed by each of the designers invited to contribute: the characteristics and location of terraces and porches were established, a uniform roof was chosen, the construction materials were determined, with brick for street facades - of the same colour as that used in the rest of zone 5 - and white plaster rendering for the interior wall surfaces, and wood for doors and window frames, painted in traditional colours, although the choice of colour for the ground floor and the entrances has been left open.

The 106 apartments are divided between two blocks, which make intensive use of the available surface area. These blocks have the task of closing off the Zone 5 area along Parallel Weg, down which the railway runs. The rest of the operation in this sector of the city consists of the construction of new apartment buildings which entirely enclose a further three blocks and combine with existing buildings to complete a fourth.

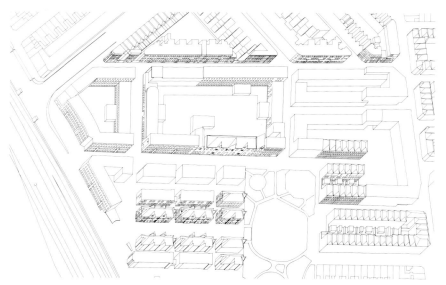

Aerial view of the site, axonometric
drawings, general plans and plans of the
different house types

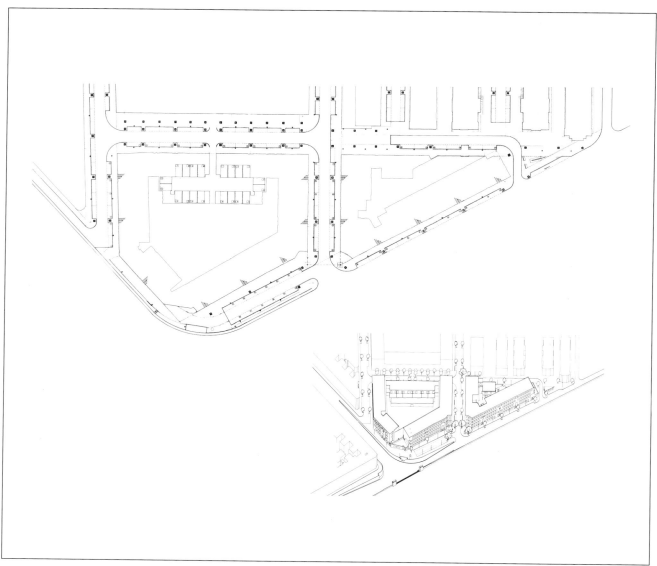

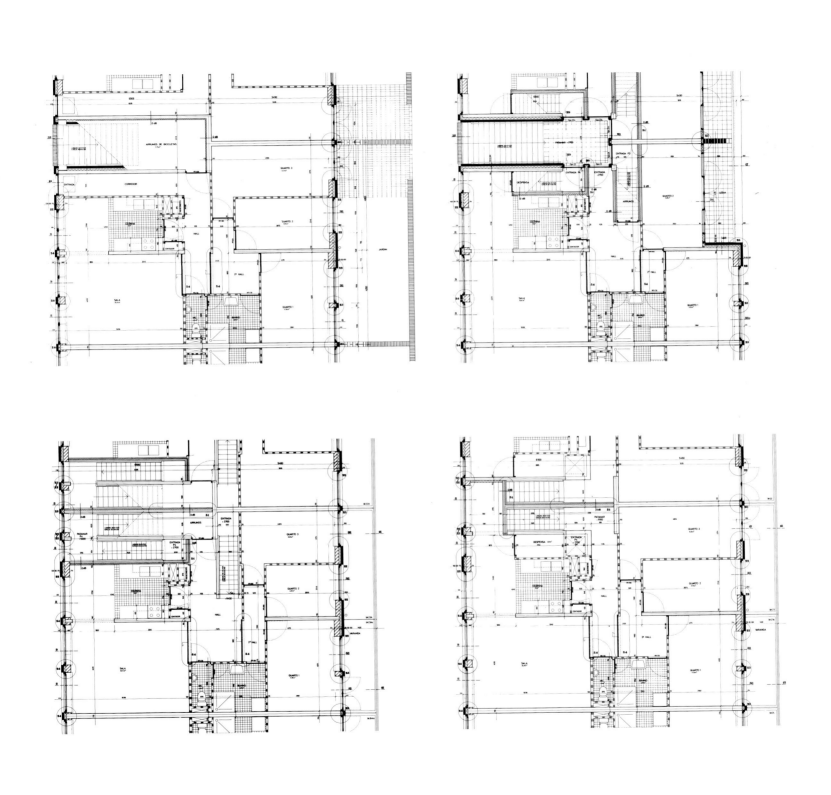

Sketch by Alvaro Siza and view of the
confluence between the two buildings

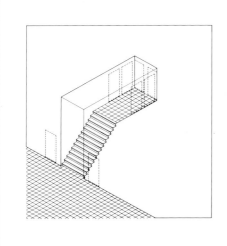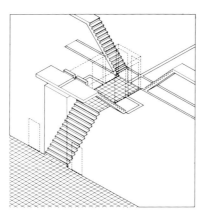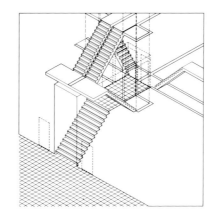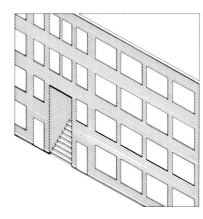

26

View of a typical access to the block and of
the internal courtyard, details of the stairs,
elevation, section and construction details

Following pages: various partial views of
the exterior of the two blocks

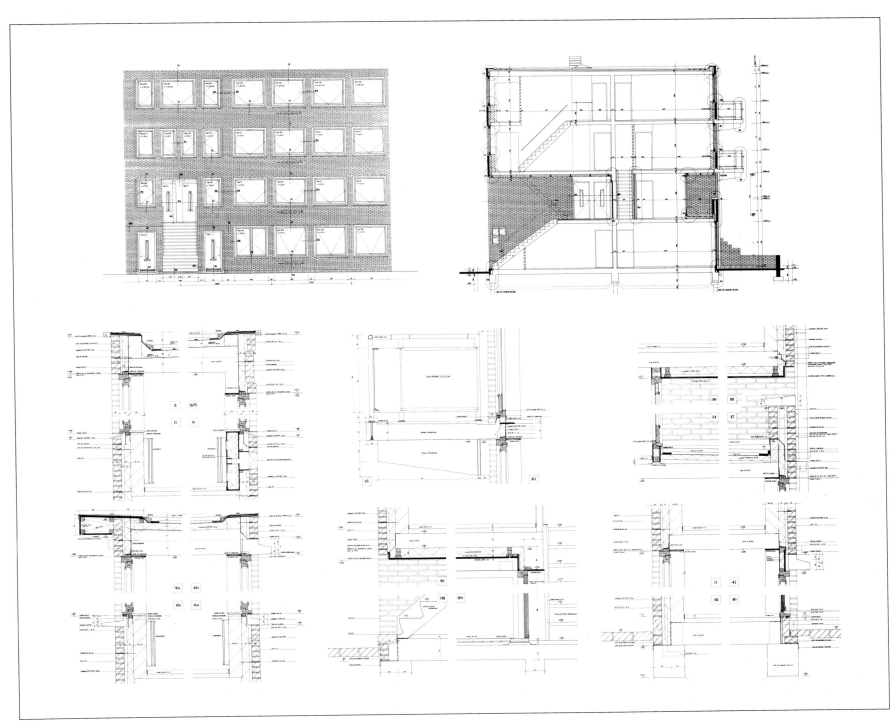

Architects: Doris & Ralph Thut

Max-Planck-Strasse
Altenerding

1983-1984   Erding, Munich (D)

This apartment building is to be found in Erding, a town of approximately 25,000 people, to the north-west of Munich.

Forming part of a new residential and industrial district on the outskirts of the traditional urban nucleus, the block is characterised by its boundary role between city and country. Although it stands some 2 km from the centre of Erding, the apartment building is surrounded by all the amenities appropriate to its urban function: a market, a school, shops and businesses and a local railway station.

Prompted initially by the Bavarian government's concern with reducing the construction costs of subsidised housing, the future tenants were encouraged to take part in the actual building of the block, leading to the relaxing of certain standards. The scheme was financed by national and regional government together, as a pilot exercise, employing the same funds normally used for the construction of subsidised housing.

The participation of the future residents was primarily concentrated on the finishing of the interiors of the apartments, where they had the choice of changing the initially open balconies and terraces into enclosed, glazed galleries, thus obtaining additional living space.

The block consists principally of duplex apartments, with four variant distributions, each of which envisages a different kind of lifestyle and use of space. These duplex apartments have surface areas of 75 m2 or 90 m2, and there are also two-room studio apartments.

The linearity of the building is interrupted at ground floor level by a passageway for cars which links up with one of the community laundries. The siting of stairs in both longitudinal and transverse relationships with the building creates differentiated spaces in the duplex apartments, with the service areas (kitchens and bathrooms) having either a closed or open relationship with the living areas.

The block, with its linear form, corresponds to the typology of the building with a communal corridor and direct entrance to each of the apartments, with a rationalised siting of the accesses on the exterior. The communal entrance is based on an open stair well, complemented by a ramp-staircase and an emergency staircase at one end of the block. In addition, each apartment is equipped with elements to give it shelter from the wind.

Conceived as a self-sufficient apartment block, the building has been equipped with a number of community facilities such as a workshop, two laundries with a drying area, an area for washing cars and a sun-terrace on the roof.

Although the interiors of the apartments were completed by the future residents themselves, we should note the intelligent study of the different materials employed in the construction, prompting an interesting approach to the composition of solutions such as that for the roof of the corridor -where sinusoidal curves combine with the longitudinal division of the wood on the lower part of the eaves - or the combining of wood laminates with stone and rendering on the facades. This innovative use of materials, together with the linear and serial development of the apartments, reinforces the sense of a modern typology for the residential building having been achieved without sacrificing the fundamentally domestic character of the private spaces.

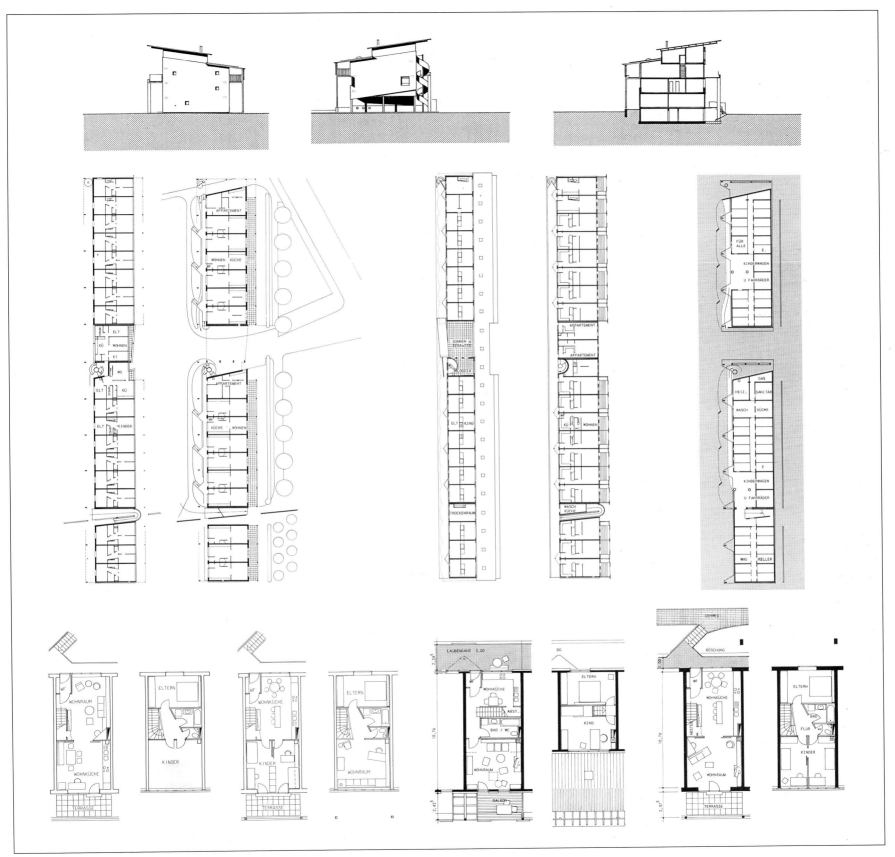

Previous pages: partial view of the main facade, general floor plans and plans of the different house types, elevations and section

Various views and details of the facades of the block

Architects: Dolf Dobbelaar, Herman de Kovel,
Paul de Vroom, DKV

Collaborator: Hans Glimmerveen

Kop St. Janshaven
Dockhaven

1986-1988   Rotterdam (NL)

This building, of considerable dimensions, is part of an urban plan drawn up by Rotterdam City Council for the revitalisation of the docks area to the south of the city by means of the creation of a total of 880 dwellings.

Situated on one of the quays of the Dockhaven harbour, opposite the park laid out on top of the sewage treatment plant, the building is the final element in a complex of residential blocks some two hundred metres in length. The main characteristic of the eleven-storey building is the series of linear glass bands which mark the rhythm of the facade. There are three complete sequences of glass, which take in 48 of the 54 duplex apartments, constituting great horizontal transparencies in the smooth facade through which the internal organisation of the apartment block is revealed. The curving end of the block, glazed to provide the entire complex with panoramic views of the city, and recalling the prow of a ship, contains the vertical circulation core which serves the galleries giving access to the individual apartments. This curving conclusion of the built volume gives a certain dynamism to the complex overlooking the Niewe Maas river, while the horizontal bands emphasise its linearity, inviting comparison with the long neighbouring block.

The members of the Dutch DKV group, Dolf Dobbelaar, Herman de Kovel and Paul de Vroom, had already previously experimented - in collaboration with Kees de Kat and the Office for Metropolitan Architecture, O.M.A. - with new proposals in the realm of housing, firmly directed at tackling the problems of difficult urban settings.

This project for subsidised housing has been thought out on the basis of the orientation and views with regard to its specific location and a precise application of the planning regulations.

The apartments are a mixture of full-sized homes and smaller 'maisonettes', combining types of dwelling of different dimensions, with the typological variants situated at either end of the block and taking advantage of their privileged position.

Inside the apartments the living area is organised so as to have these rooms opening onto the two facades: the main bedroom looks out onto the park, while the dining room, with its small pantry or 'conservatory', looks towards the port. Thanks to the bands of glazing running along the front of this space and the bedrooms, the dining area enjoys extensive views despite being situated in the interior of the apartment. At the same time, the disposition of the 'conservatory' allows a circular itinerary through the different parts of the house.

The system of accesses employed here deserves particular attention, with a vertical service core of lifts and stairs which we might define as public in character alternating with galleries which act as private dining areas giving access to the interior of the apartment. In this way it is possible to appreciate the advantages of accessibility proportioned by the glazed corridors.

The problem of the wind posed by the building's situation on the dockside has been resolved by means of the concave form and the prism-shaped residential nucleus which rises up behind it, while full advantage has been taken of the sunlight, and the views are much improved by the building's transparency.

The construction is based on the assembly of precast concrete elements, clad with an exterior thermal skin, with pale green rendering on the side facing the park and pale grey on the side facing the port.

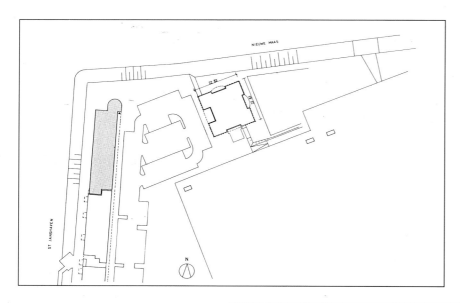
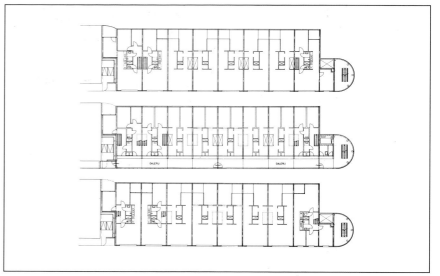
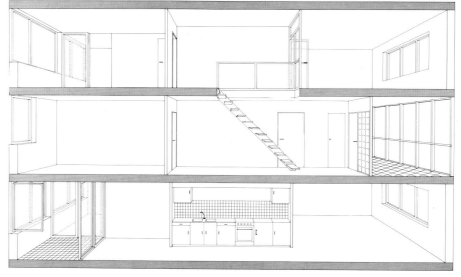

38

Previous pages: site plan, floor plans,
sectional perspective, view of the model,
perspective and view of the access corridor
to the apartments

View of the facade with the access
corridors to the apartments

41

Architects: Henk Döll, Erick van Egeraat, Francine Houben,
Chris de Weijer, MECANOO ARCHITEKTEN

Hillekop

Afrikaanderwisk
Rotterdam South

1985-1989   Rotterdam (NL)

To the south of Rotterdam, in the zone known as the 'African Quarter' - whose origins and original urban development date from the 19th century - on a site running along the left bank of the world's largest industrial harbour (Rijnhaven), stands the Hillekop complex. Situated at the end of one of the quays which marks the boundary between city and port, the complex comprises a total of 197 apartments, equipped with a community centre, with the railway line to one side and the raised tracks of the metro and a navegable canal to the other.

The project declined to create a built-up city block, choosing instead to make use of what the context could provide: the scheme conceived of three differentiated buildings, of which the tall west-facing tower is the outstanding volume, in such a way as to offer panoramic views of the port and along the railway line. A long, sinuous building - following the line of the elevated metro - serves as its base and point of connection with the surrounding urban context, while a third, L-shaped building concludes and closes off an existing city block from its junction with the party wall. The contrast created by the disparity between the heights of the different buildings, with their silhouettes outlined against the open space of the harbour, is strikingly evident.

The tower, which fans out in such a way that the perception of its spatial quality changes as the visitor approaches, contains a hundred apartments laid out with an average of six to a floor. These share a common entrance, with a grand vestibule which also communicates with the service and maintenance areas; at the same time, the interior of each apartment, in following the concave form of the skin of the facade, opens towards the port, acting as a semi-public viewing platform, while the rear of the tower makes absolutely no contact with the ferry terminal behind it. The block with the double curve is six storeys high, containing 80 single-level apartments, with access provided by means of an external lift tower housing two lifts.

In this way a vertical communications core is created, which, moreover, takes advantage of the cutting-back of the facade at fifth-floor level to develop a corridor which makes itself evident on the exterior as a

lighter element in contrast with the solidity and monotony of the block. Thanks to its S-shaped curve, the block adapts to the line of the main street, opening up by means of a portico which signals the entrance to the urban gateway onto Afrikaanswijk; at either end, the head and tail of the block are bounded by landscaped squares.
The third block, on the corner of Hillelaanstraat, has a height of four storeys; this volume completes the urban composition in joining on to the existing city block.

Dutch building regulations, which provide for the possibility of flooding as a result of changes in the level of the water in the dykes - Hilledijk - of the Meuse, have directly conditioned the form of the stepped terraces.

Mecanoo, a team of four young architects, is part of the new generation which is revitalising the Dutch architectural scene. The group's work is characterised by the use of images drawn from the recent past - the Modern Movement - which they interpret in terms of present-day construction techniques. The choice of materials, revealing professional rigour and sensibility in a new urban context, together with the typologies employed, make Hillekop a highly interesting residential complex.

The scheme's intervention on the quayside, in the form of the three individual buildings, is reminiscent of a time when the creation of urban spaces and sectors of the city - as in the German Siedlungs and the Austrian Hoffs - was conceived on the basis of the study of the building's internal or external circulation schemes, the latter connecting with the streets and avenues which articulate the position of the blocks, here finished with industrial cladding.

Various views of the exterior of the two blocks

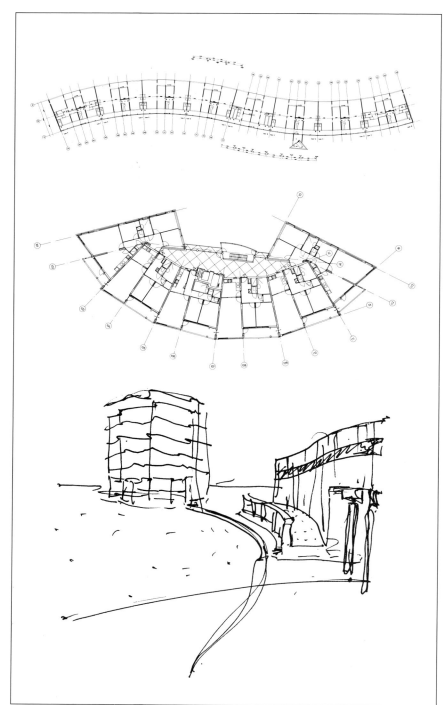

Model, site plan, plans, sketch, elevations
and sections

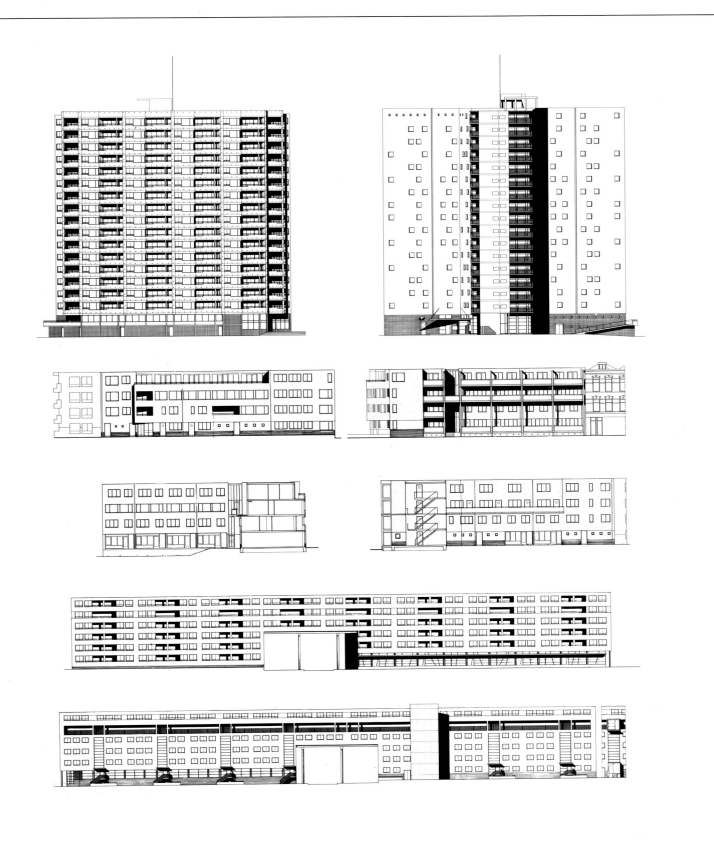

Architects: Aldo Rossi, Gianni Braghieri

Collaborators: Grötzebach, Plessow, Ehlers, Christopher Stead, Jay Johnson

Block 10 IBA
Südliche Friedrichstadt

1981-1988   Berlin (D)

In 1981, Aldo Rossi and his team came first in the Berlin IBA's competition for the design of a residential block to complete a macroblock, known as Block 10.

The block has been approached on the urban scale, recognising the city in its entirety as the main premise, aligning itself with various different axes, and compacted with the already constructed elements in order to create a better environment for urban living.
To this end, porticoes have been constructed all around the perimeter of the block giving onto the street, in an effort at forging a union between the existing buildings and the new scheme. The courtyard in the interior has been landscaped as a sheltered garden which can nevertheless be seen by passersby as they walk along the street. The continuity of the plane of the facade and the regularity of height throughout its entire length, offering views interrupted only by the gardens, allows Rossi to simultaneously reflect the scale of the old city and the new, conceived as a single whole.
The urban gateways in the middle of the blocks and their lift towers, which reveal themselves on the exterior as glazed pinnacles, are the elements which personalize the building here.

Aldo Rossi has erected here the great white column, that reference to be found in other of his projects and design schemes which is constructed here for the first time; found in the classics, too (Filarete in Venice or Alberti in Mantua), as a sign of an urban nucleus, of the historic life of the city. The column on the corner allows the blocks to divide at the precise point where they turn, serving as a marking sign. The rear facades are individualised by the use of glass and copper sheeting on the roof, and form a wall which is independent of the volume of the block, bringing out onto the exterior the galleries which give access to the different floors.

For Rossi, the personal inventiveness and the inherent quality of his construction are not to be put forward solely on the private scale, but also on the level or tackling the architectural and urban design problems of the city as a whole.

In the light of this, the architect allows a figurative, almost pictorial element to be discerned in the background of his constructions, a quality evident in work in a variety of different contexts. In postulating this abstract formalisation of architecture in a book of key significance for the history of architecture - his *Autobiografia Scientifica* - Rossi situated himself at the forefront of the movement known as 'L'Architettura Razionale'. The city is, for Rossi, a resource capable of suggesting new readings of the urban space which make for the use of grand columns, tall plinths in the facade and geometric elements.

Rossi seems to think and design exactly what he draws, and it is the act of constructing which is charged with the task of giving material substance to the drawn reality. The pictorial figuration (we should bear in mind his constant references to the Italian painter De Chirico), surveying and recreating itself in inspirational themes, seems to tie up perfectly with the architectonic execution which he draws and simultaneosly constructs.

Thus the relationship between the project and the materials it employs: brick is an element used in much of his work, allowing the architecture to be perceived by means of the addition of each little component part, one by one.

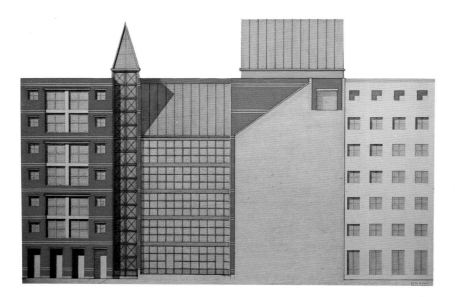

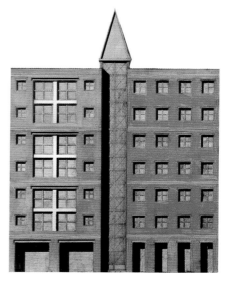

Coloured elevations and view of the street facade and the facade on the interior courtyard

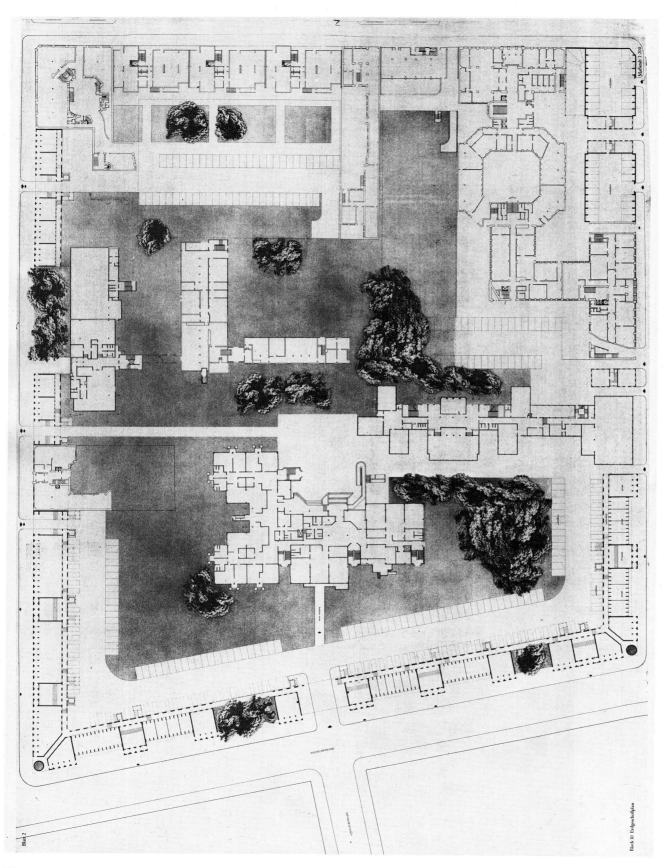

Following pages: general and partial views
of the rear facade

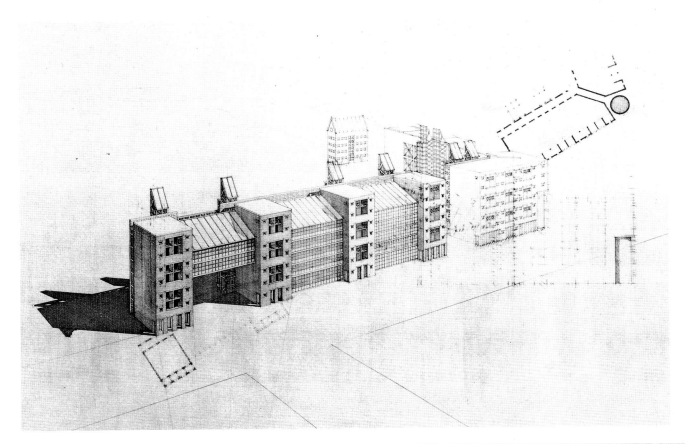

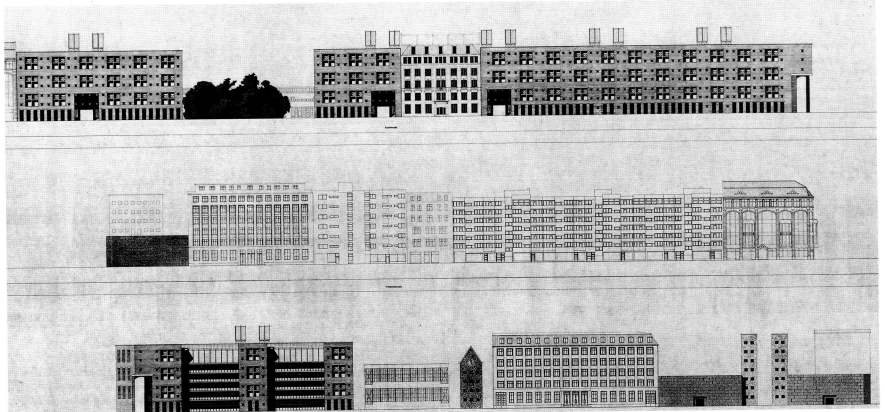

55

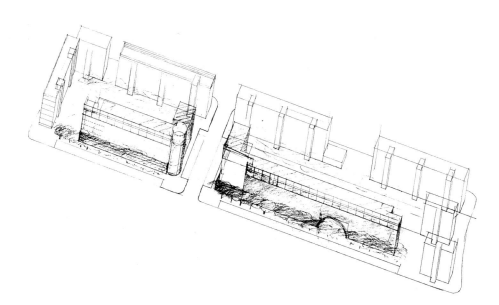

Architects: Guillermo Vázquez Consuegra

Collaborators: Carmen Ortiz, Ramón Romero, Ricardo Alario

Polígono Los Corrales

Calle de Barbate

1986-1991   Cádiz (E)

This publicly funded development of 180 low-cost apartments is being built on two vacant plots on the Polígono de Los Corrales estate, constructed in the 60s in the disorderly urban isthmus of Cádiz, outside the walls of the historic city. The form and situation of the plots, together with the local building regulations - with a classification as 'Ordenación Abierta', allowing considerable flexibility - applying to them, made it possible to divide the built area into two great linear blocks, which undergo successive modification in the course of their section, configuring a system of continuous occupation along calle Barbate.

The blocks, of 62 m and 116 m in length, respectively, adopt an L-shaped arrangement in order to emphasise the corners of the buildings, while at the same time allowing the precise configuration of the public space in the interior of the plots, with two paved squares lined with rows of pines and orange trees.

Block 1, as it is known, adopts the double-bay apartment as its typological basis, with the aim of making maximum use of the floor plan, occupying as it does the entire 10 metres of usable depth. Block 2 is a more complex organism, structured in two volumes set parallel to one another - the inner of which has six floors of duplex apartments, accepting its subsidiary role in relation to the main block - and connected by two metal bridges, between them composing a semi-private pedestrian precinct leading to one of the squares. In this way, the project sets itself up as an alternative to the compact block with internal light wells.

This basically linear block successively entertains a series of formal adaptations deriving from the various different constraints imposed by its great length. The projection of the four upper floors out over calle Barbate, at the end of the block, is a gesture which gives a singular formal character to the building's conclusion; the gallery apartments as a direct response to the foregoing decision, or the great roofed hallway giving access to the two main doors - which, moreover, serve to communicate the pedestrian street with calle Barbate - should be seen as mechanisms for the clearer expression of this idea. The heads of the two blocks are distinguished by means of a quite different formal treatment, curving with a slight inflection and establishing a dialogue between themselves which ensures their common urban unity.

The unitary treatment of the long facades, to which the utilisation of a single type of opening adds a good deal, the absence of terraces and the continuous bands of gold-coloured tiles between windows together contribute to the creation of a powerful visual element which establishes a new identity in the midst of the rather chaotic urban fabric.

The belvedere looking out over the bay, at the vertex of Block 1, crowned by a balcony bounded by a curving glass wall which is reached by way of an open ramp, is a reference by analogy - free of formal imitation - to the watchtowers which dot the urban landscape of Cádiz, at the same time as it contributes to the objective of providing this poorly ordered part of the city's outskirts with a clear sign of identity.

The construction is based on traditional elements such as brick and 'in situ' reinforced concrete. Two different solutions have been adopted for the roofs: a flat roof, which can be walked on, and a curving roof (a sandwich of three layers of anodised lacquered sheet metal) for the second, parallel, residential block.

General floor plan and various exterior
views of the two blocks

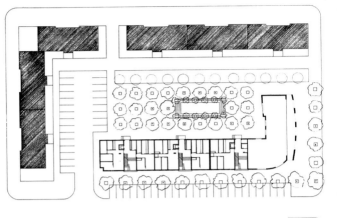
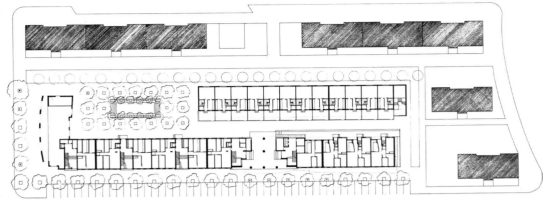

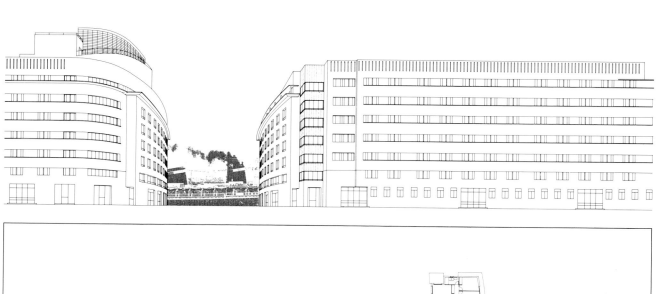

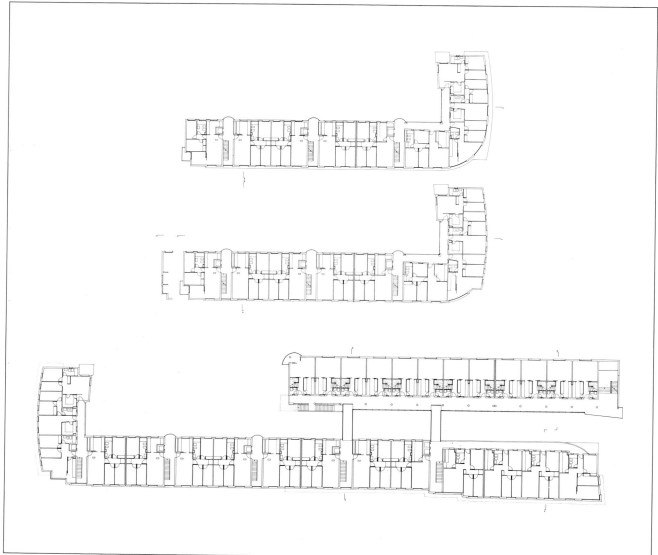

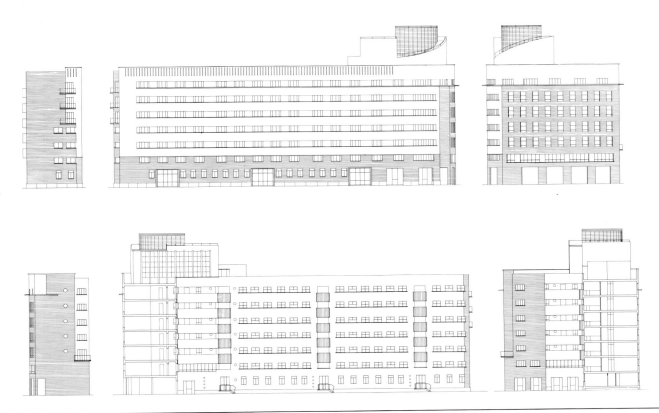

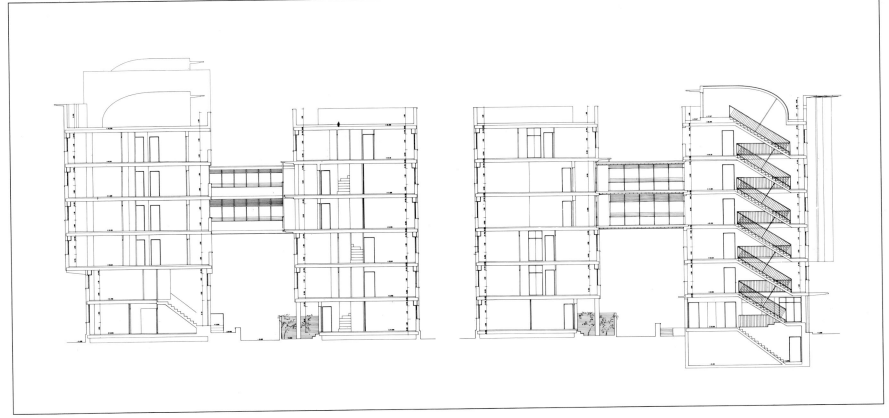

Perspective and various views of the
exterior and the access galleries serving
the apartments

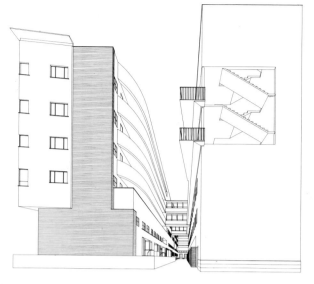

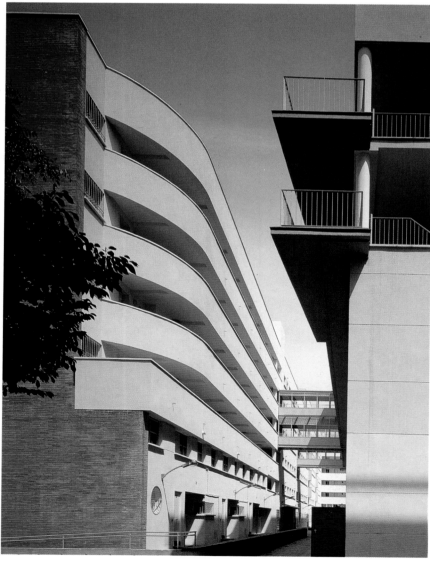

Architects: Jean Nouvel et Associés, Jean Marc Ibos,
Jean-Rémy Negre, Frédéric Chambon

Nemausus 1

Rue de Vistre / Avenue du Général Leclerc

1985-1987   Nîmes (F)

Within the context provided by an extensive programme for the construction and refurbishment of rent-controlled housing undertaken by Nîmes city council, this first building of 114 apartments is developed in an industrial zone to the south-west of the city, between the southern ring road, rue de Vistre and the avenue General Léclérc.

Nemausus I seeks to provide an alternative to the typical approach to subsidised housing, which usually implies a very limited programme, poor finishing and desolate surroundings.

In the first place, the scheme sets out to take fullest possible advantage of the usable surface area of the built space. This has been achieved by locating the stairs on the exterior of the building, by reducing the communal spaces which are generally little used and by rationalising the floor plan in an additive series of rectangles, without corners or recessed spaces. Nouvel's scheme marks a change from the normally pessimistic tone of subsidised housing, offering an alternative in which the quality of the space, the materials employed and the relationship with the exterior are far removed from the general run of public sector building. At the same time, the adoption of industrial techniques and the use of fast, easily assembled patent construction materials, chosen straight from the catalogue, have allowed the necessary economic viability.

There are 17 different house types, all laid out at right angles to the line of the block, which thus gives them a double orientation and lets them take advantage of the communal corridors, which serve as porches when the doors of the apartment are fully opened. The use of perforated sheet metal for the balustrades of the terraces adds to the visual transparency, relating the surrounding landscaped area to the building itself and increasing the safety factor thanks to the oblique section.

Finally, the screen of tall, leafy trees which surrounds the complex shelters it from the heavy traffic on the ring road and sensitively defines the relationship with the parking spaces at ground floor level. The building is raised up off the ground, freeing the space beneath it for use as an airy, naturally-illuminated car park.

The building's construction is based on a reinforced concrete structure with a rectangular grid 5 m across and 12 m deep, repeated with a variety of different surface finishes. All of the materials used are industrial, making for great ease of assembly and a minimum of subsequent maintenance. Thus, the doors onto the terraces which make it possible to entirely open the facade to the exterior space are the same as those to be found in garages for large vehicles, the metal stairs are those used in the steel industry; the industrial flooring is of the continuous type to be seen in airports or department stores and the PVC sunshades are widely used in agriculture.

Nemausus I presents itself as a manifesto for a new style of social housing, in which industry is called on to provide the technology, so as to offer more extensive, better quality spaces for the same budget.

The references to the machine formalised by the building are everywhere in evidence, with the roof, the terraces and the transparency of the ground floor level continually alluding to the aesthetic myths of ship and plane; references to which the lighting at night - employing marine signal beacons - gives radical expression.

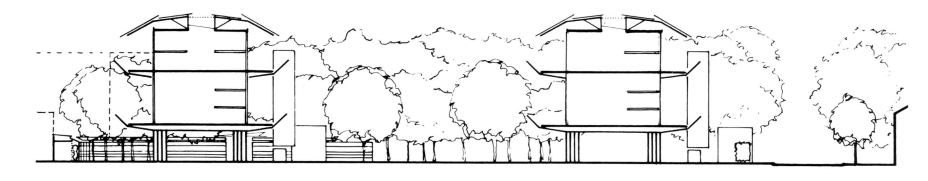

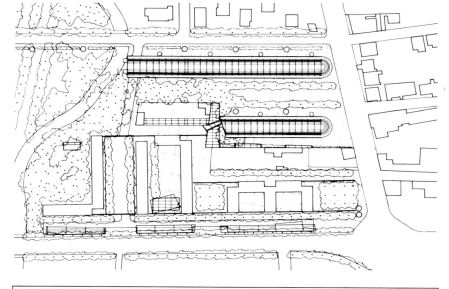

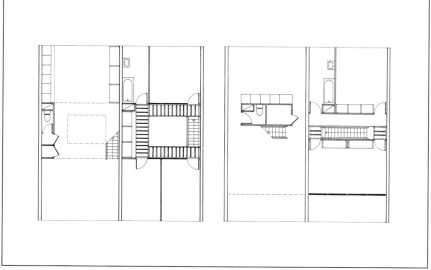

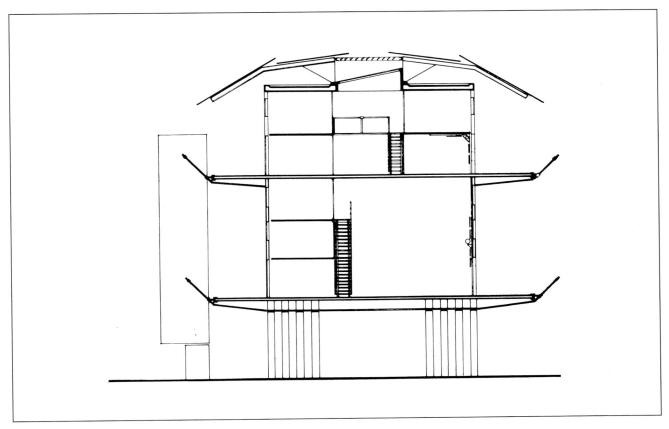

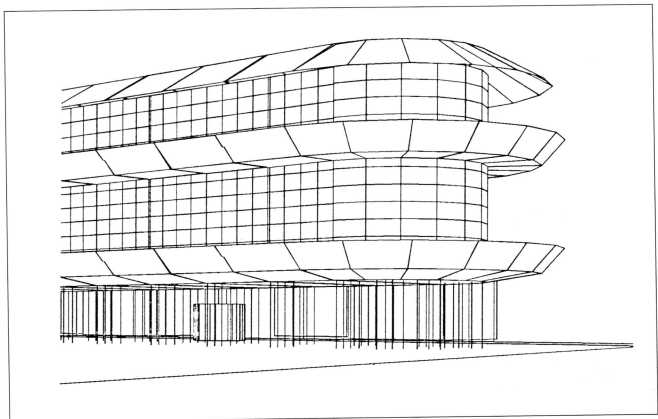

70

Various views of the car park, access galleries to the houses and their interiors

Architects: Bernardo Font-Brescia, Laurinda Spear,
Hervin A.R. Romney, Arquitectonica International Corporation

The Imperial

Brickwell Avenue, Biscayne Bay

1979-1983   Miami, Florida (US)

Overlooking the Bay of Biscayne, this skyscraper apartment building has one hundred and sixty-two apartments spread over its thirty-one floors, plus three floors of underground car parking for 330 vehicles. The building also contains five duplex homes on the ground floor and a two-storey studio penthouse. In addition, the project includes a swimming pool, a tennis-court, a fitness centre and a wide walkway leading to a small islet in the waters of the Bay.

As in other schemes by the husband and wife team of Bernardo Fort-Brescia and Laurinda Spear, together with Hervin A.R. Romney, this residential skyscraper reveals a certain monumental, 'film set' quality - apparent even in the name of the building - derived from its origins and location, alongside a markedly populist character.
Miami is a young city, less than a hundred years old, and still growing, with its roots in the twin function which defines its character: leisure and business. Now, as since its origins as a colony for Cuban emigrés, its evolution is in the direction of a tropical metropolis, its image characterised by pastel tones and smooth forms. In the light of this, the building's colour, its grand scale and the evident metaphor of a large window opening onto the bay and the ocean are perfectly in line with the great American tradition in building.

The residential skyscraper aspires to the status of a small, self-contained vertical city, with a life of its own, at a distance from the street and the urban grid.
The essence of the way of life in the apartments is communal, with many of its facilities intended for the joint use of the tenants.
There can be no doubt that Arquitectonica have managed to endow many of their buildings with an interest that goes beyond technical considerations of design, and it may well be that this 'film set' element is responsible for their being used as locations in numerous TV commercials and films. *The Atlantis, The Palace and The Imperial* itself are good illustrations of this impact.

The building has the form of a cuboid, from which an enormous wall of red brick seems to hang in defiance of gravity, with its corners, angled towards the bay to create a solid screen, functioning as an opaque wall to bestow the necessary degree of privacy on the rooftop penthouse. To the south, an opening defined by the void created in the block itself takes the form of a great doorway, virtually an atrium, eight storeys tall, which breaks the volume of the building and exposes the vestibule of the complex to public view.
Two additional elements complete the composition: a striking cobalt blue structure formed by the sun lounges of three of the dwellings, which act as shade-giving elements accentuating their 125 metres of length, and a free, curving form, electric blue in colour, which completes the two-storey studio on the roof of the skyscraper.

This architecture, which has probably come to constitute the built expression of a certain culture, bases its principles on the commercial promotion of the building as a symbol, and on the fragmentation of elementary forms by means of light and colour, representing the combination of Anglo-Saxon culture and a Hispanic way of life and customs, respectively. Their buildings are part of a process which has converted the principles of the Modern Movement into a style, making of the skeleton of the structure and its outer skin an expressive collage of contrasts in which the intense colours and pure geometries seem to generate themselves spontaneously.

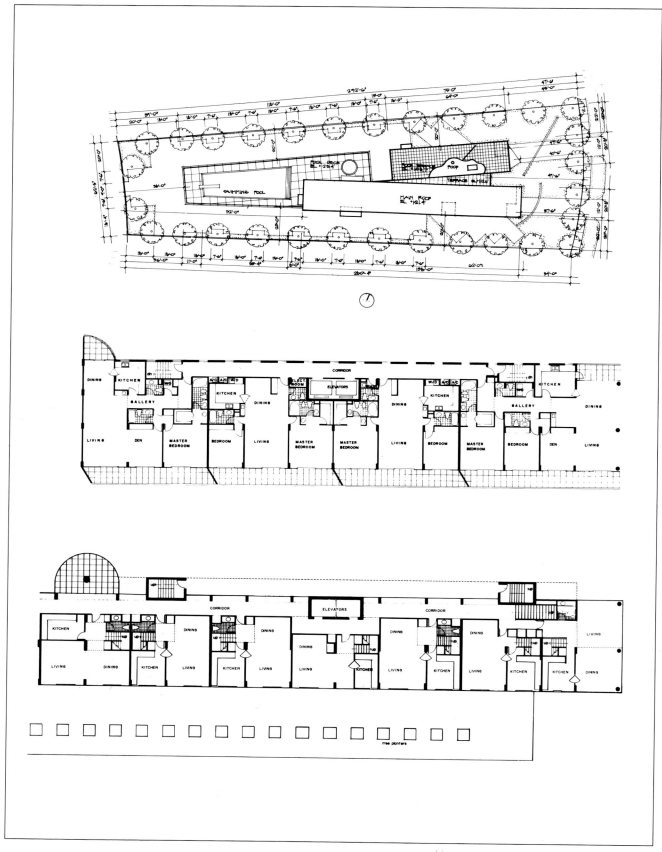

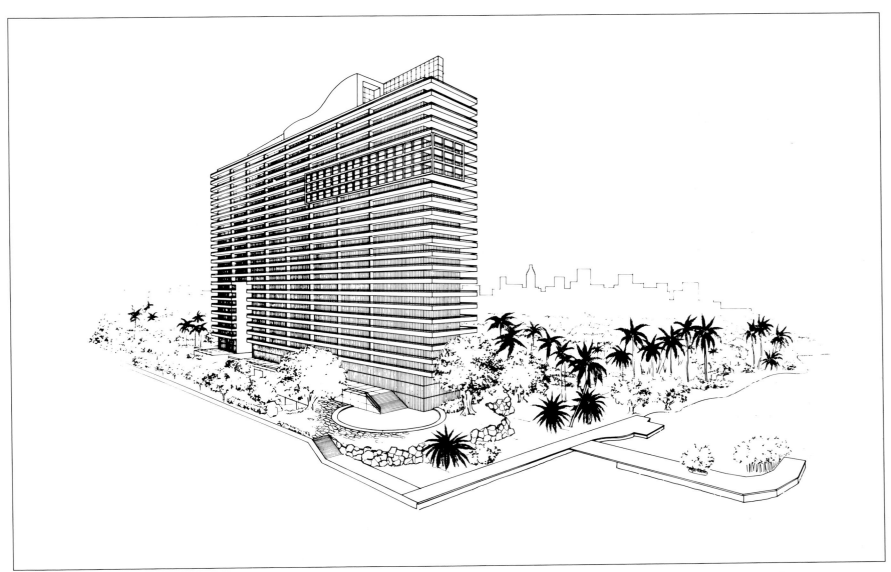

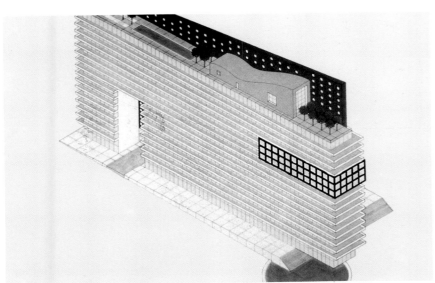

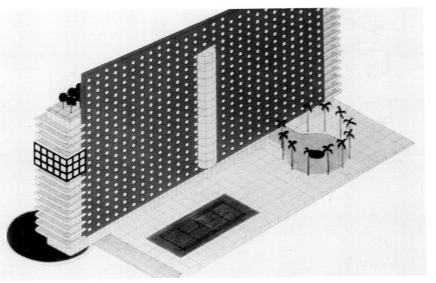

Various views of the exterior

Architect: Daniel Liebeskind

City Edge IBA
24 Am Karlsbad, Flottwellstrasse

1987   Berlin (D)

The building rises up along the length of Flottwellstrasse, linking together Blocks 228/240, as they are known, in a single urban structure for a variety of functions, residential, commercial and public use.

The project seeks to demonstrate, in planning terms, the viability of using the traditional structure of the Berlin apartment building while at the same time overcoming its physical limitations through the creation of a new scale and way of living for the Berlin of the future.

The block is organised around a pedestrian walkway which is gradually modified from a historic boulevard to the avenue which marks out the urban structure of the future city.

The model explains the building from every angle and in all its aspects. This is made out of scraps of paper from architects' drawings, bibles, maps, telephone directories, banknotes ..., anything which can be readily cut up and incorporated into the volume.

The plan of the project clearly reveals the basic ideas behind the complexity and sophistication of the residential block in relation to the urban exterior.
It is important to note the way in which any conceptual formalisation can give rise to new approaches to the grouping together of dwellings and spaces with various different functions.
The drawings and the model give an idea of what might be conceived of as future ways of living in a residential block.

The project was unanimously voted winner of the IBA (the International Architecture Exhibition promoted by the Berlin senate) competition in 1987. The building it represents has a length of 450 metres, 10 metres deep and 20 metres high, rising obliquely at an angle of 6 degrees to reach a height of 56 metres.

It is scarcely coincidence that the point of origin of the foundations of this architectonic object should be just opposite number 24, Am Karlsbad, where the architect Mies van der Rohe had his office from

1918-1938, now a public park. The area equivalent to numbers 11 to 15, Am Karlsbad, will provide parking places for 200 vehicles on two underground levels.

The building crosses over Lützowstrasse, with a clearance of 6 metres to allow pedestrian and vehicular traffic to pass underneath it, to arrive at Pohlstrasse, the next street, where the underground railway comes up out of the ground to pass right through the apartment block.
The vertical circulation has been transformed into 'big wheels', revolving to give access from the ground to the topmost floor; every 55 metres there is a core of ramps, stairs and doors to interconnect all the floors which is also a nucleus for large areas of leisure facilities such as art galleries and cinemas.

In spite of the repetitive rhythm of the structure, the apartments have flexibility of use and maintenance, leaving each of the residents free to lay out the interior in line with their own needs.

The drawings shown are no more than preliminary sketches, yet they give enough information for engineers and quantity surveyors to have worked out initial studies for construction. Ove Arup and his team have taken up the challenge of giving material form to this remarkable scheme, which will undoubtedly call for more detailed analysis once it has gone into construction.

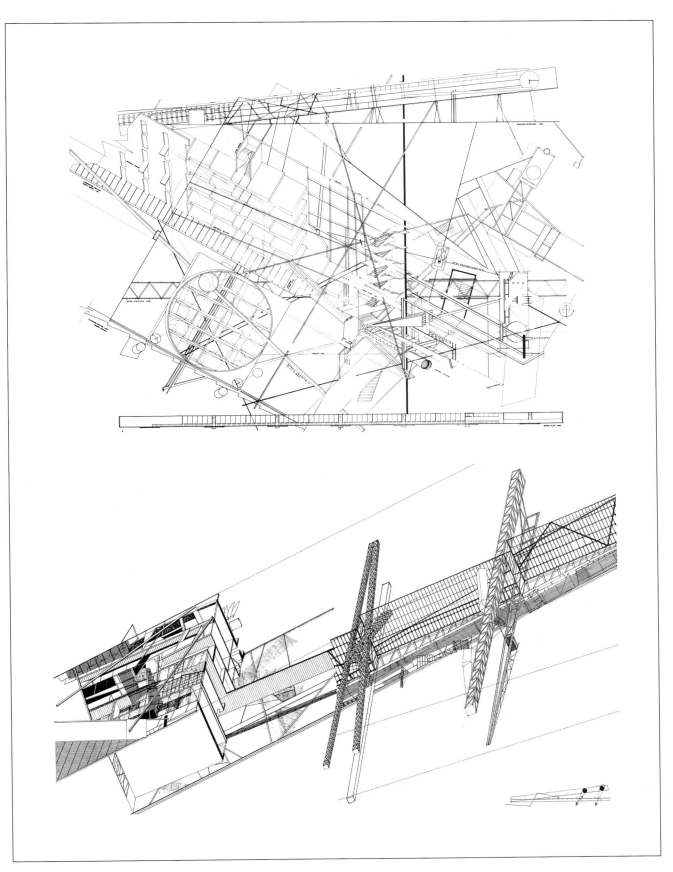

Architects: Roger Diener, Marcus Diener, Diener & Diener,
Massimo Corradi, Lorenzo Goetg, Dieter Righetti, Emil Rysler

Collaborators: Wolfgang Schett, Christian Stamm

Housing & Office Complex

**Riehenring-Amerbachstrasse 82-85/
Efringerstrasse-Allschwilerstrasse**

1980-1985   Basle (CH)

The planned blocks, in a U-formation, are situated in one of the industrial areas of the city of Basle, laid out as the continuation, in general terms, of the morphology to be seen in the neighbouring blocks.
The programme is centred on the combination of subsidised housing with offices and shops, parking spaces for cars and the opening up of a new passageway.
The intervention is divided over three clearly differentiated facades, each giving onto a different street, consisting of a complex of three- and five-room apartments which can be easily extended through the conversion of annex spaces into living areas.

As in other projects by these architects in Basle, their aim is to endow their buildings with a certain character which draws them closer to their urban context, up to the point where it forms a part of their very structure. Accordingly, the formation of this type of building is to be understood in terms of its relationships with its surroundings and the underlying demands this contains. The fact that each of the blocks incorporates different alternatives, combining public and private uses, adds experimentation with the urban space and its connection with the apartments to the contradictions inherent in the setting.
The blocks, presented as adaptations to the urban reality, declare their receptivity to their specific conditions of use and place, while being perceived as part of a whole: the city.

Roger and Marcus Diener belong to the younger generation of Swiss architects, manifestly concerned with adapting to certain specifically local traditions of construction and with an effective implementation of the programme. The evocation of images of a modernism still close at hand in architectural history, combined with formal discretion, together lead their buildings to express themselves with a clarity which renounces any kind of concession to historicism.
The unity of the complex, with its determination to avoid the spectacular, does not diminish the individuality of each of its component parts, characterised by different typologies linked together by the specificity of their setting.

The apartments are laid out transversely, running from facade to facade and offering generous interior spaces which make clear reference to the structure used to support the building. The configuration of the dwellings allows for the rooms in the interior to be made larger or smaller in keeping with the changes in the users' circumstances and way of life.
The two corners of the U-shaped complex are set aside for stores, shops and offices, articulating the larger dimensions of the blocks as they turn to align themselves with the street axes. The building is stepped back to accomodate the stairs, creating courtyards which face out onto the street, while the terrace serves as a communal area for sunbathing.
At the same time, the kitchens are interiorised along Efringerstrasse, allowing the balconies to run in horizontal sequence the entire length of the facade.
The new pedestrian precinct adjacent to the building narrows where it reaches a roofed garage, providing a netball court as a recreational area.
Views from the internal access are given emphasis by the asymmetrical expansion of the meetings between blocks, culminating in the superimposition of the eaves of the concrete roof.

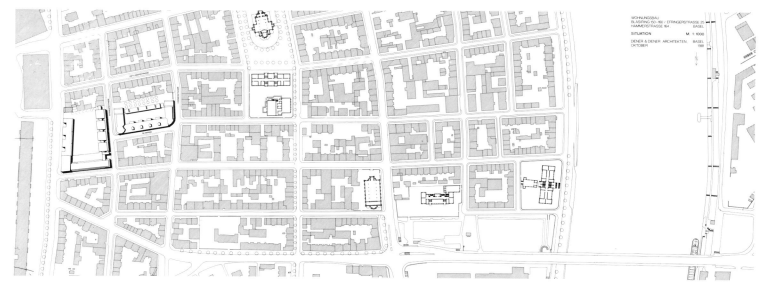

WOHNUNGSBAU
BLASIRING 150–160 / EFRINGERSTRASSE 25
HAMMERSTRASSE 164   BASEL

SITUATION   M. 1:1000

DIENER & DIENER ARCHITEKTEN. BASEL
OKTOBER   1981

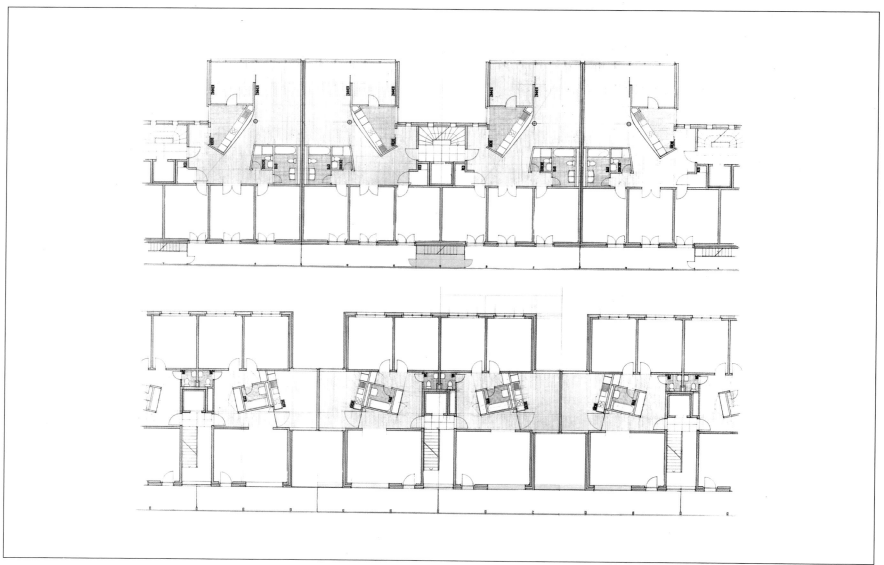

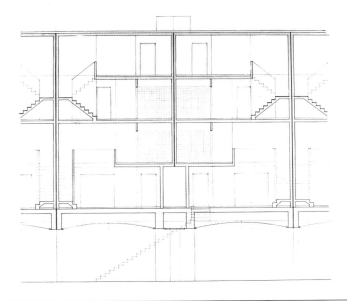

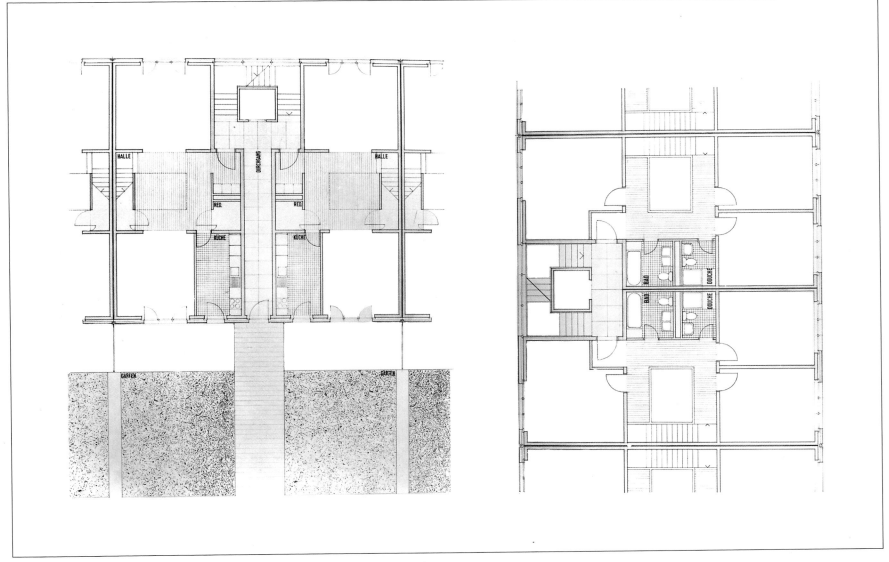

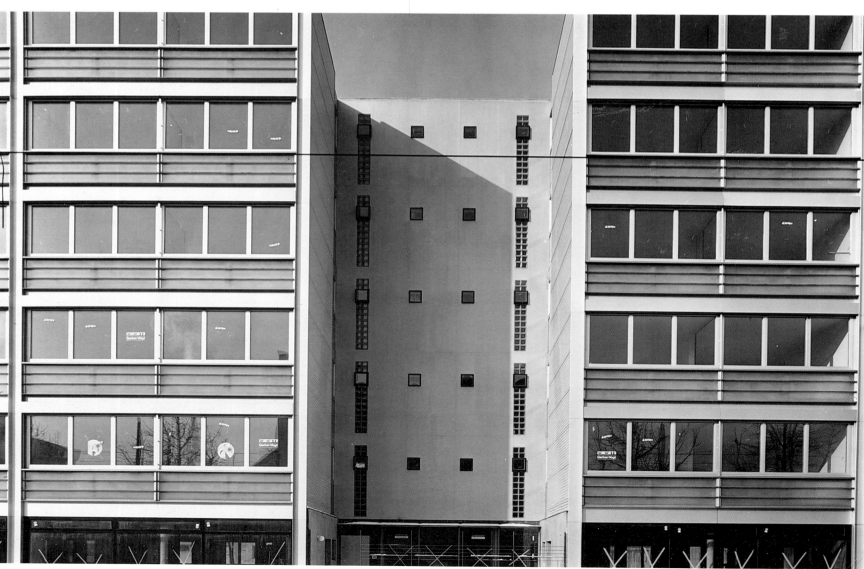

View of the roof and the two facades

Architect: Oswald Mathias Ungers

Collaborators: E.V. Branca, J.V. Brandt, K.L. Dietzsch, B. Taha

Block 1 IBA

Köthener Strasse 35-37 / Bernburger Strasse 16-18

1981-1987   Berlin (D)

Block number 1, built at the confluence of three streets, which should form the urban gateway for eastern access to the Friedrichvorstadt district, is only one part of the scheme initially submitted to the ideas competition held by the International Architecture Exhibition, the IBA, in 1982.

The block's programme consists in achieving a mixed set of uses (such as housing, offices and leisure activities) at the same time as it meets the planning objective of reconstituting a built structure in keeping with the character of the site. This derives its interest from the fact that it once formed part of the boundary between an area densely populated before the war and the Potsdam railway station, soon to be transformed into a park.
The reconstruction of the plan and scale of the city, replacing its historical limit, is defined by the addition of eight small, autonomous blocks, their dimensions determined by the surviving pre-war buildings. These dimensions are fixed as a modular 40 x 40 m unit with the idea of transforming the structure of buildings with a courtyard into a single, unified scheme. The addition of the autonomous volumes makes for permeability of passage and views in all directions, at the same time delimiting little urban areas in the interior of the built block. The different volumes are isolated from one another at ground, first and second floor level, while their upper three floors are connected by means of glazed galleries which act as bridges.

The 45 units, with their extensive surface areas, were designed for large families who would be likely to make use of the playing field and spacious landscaped zone in the vicinity. The apartments on the lower floors have a special identity, functioning more like terraced private houses, with their own direct access at ground level, while the upper floors are reached by way of the stairs at the corners of the blocks.

All of the apartments have glazed galleries or 'loggias' two storeys high.

The courtyard functions as the centre and establishes the identity of the building, and the triple-height openings allow the adjacent exterior spaces to communicate, relating the public space of the street with the interior of the communal courtyard.

Stasis, solemnity and a certain monumental quality are the principles manifest in the potent geometry - the form of the cube - employed in the evolution of the project, which, together with the materials used, gives an austerity and severity to an architecture which seeks to create habitable forms on the basis of order and automatism.

The strict geometry, conceived in terms of clear organisation, serves in the design of precise, pure volumes, bodies whose form and content are one, composing an absolute entity.
Oswald Mathias Ungers, in concentrating his researches on the residential phenomenon and the relationship of the fragment to the whole, of the house with the city, has defined the use of the perfect cube in rules which embody the expression of its very significance: 'the question of beautiful buildings in which people can live comfortably merges with the building's obedience to the pure and private iconology of its designer.'

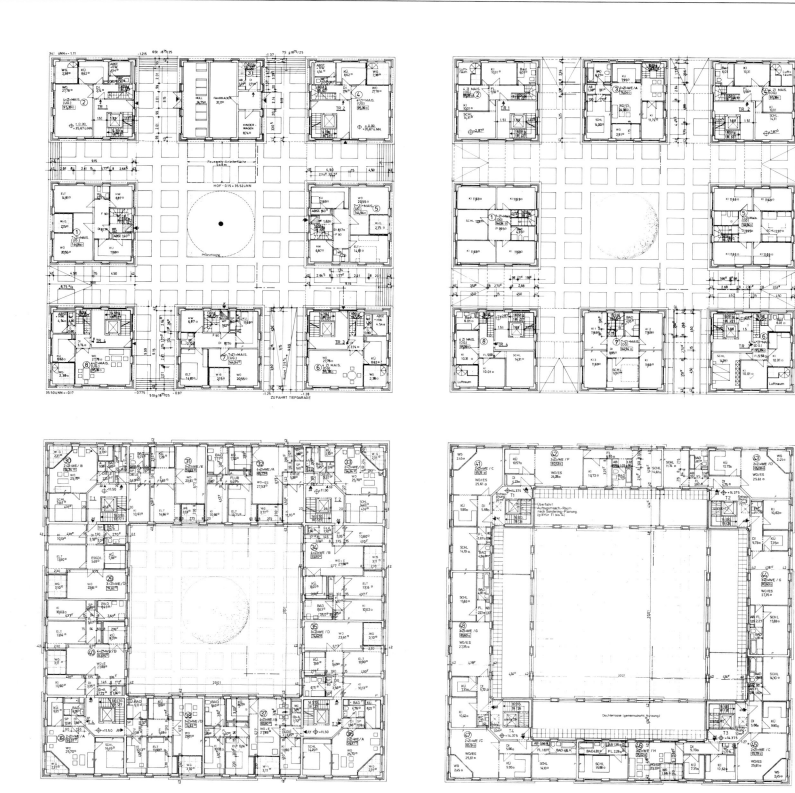

90

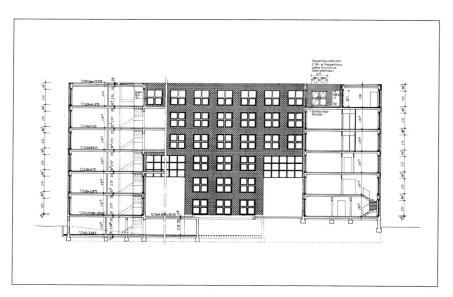

92

Previous pages: plans, elevation and view of the exterior

Section, axonometric drawing and various views of the block

Architects: Colquhoun, Miller + Partners

Collaborators: John Hunter, Shinichi Tomoe

Single Person Flats
119 Hornsey Lane

1979-1980   Haringey, London NG (GB)

Standing on a narrow strip of land, surrounded by tall residential buildings, on top of a hill with views of the city of London to north and south, this tower block of 34 apartments, with complementary communal services, was designed by two people. The site was formerly occupied by a group of old villas, which have progressively made way for small but tall apartment blocks.

The importance of the highly individual programme, of the construction techniques employed, of the relationship of a new building to the context of an already existing reality - formal, spatial, cultural, historical - the use of ramps to serve the main access to the building, ... are some of the criteria adopted by the architects, whose origins are to be found in the Team X of the 60s. Language, function and structure are here raised from being merely secondary characteristics of the building to become its substance.

Alan Colquhoun, from his position as architectural theorist and critic, authority on Le Corbusier and the Modern Movement, and John Miller have here taken the urban context as something 'necessary', seeking to emphasise the continuity with the garden city tradition in British architecture, a town interspersed with landscaped areas and public spaces. Far removed from empty formalisms and unattainable utopias, the proposed scheme sets out to be coherent with its final appearance without losing the human dimension which relates it to the occupants. A window is no longer identified with a fissure between two solids, but becomes the object of an analysis of its complex uses and significations, although these undoubtedly derive from the historical tradition or from certain construction techniques.

The British empiricism which provides an explanation for the work of Colquhoun and Miller determines the design of the plan in a building that is austere, with openings in only two of its facades, yet which nevertheless seeks to put forward a specific vision of the programme to be developed: housing for married couples with no children or for two single people sharing the same apartment; a simple programme handled with realism.

The tower block, with a total of nine floors, stands on a site very typical of the outskirts of a British radial city, with an extremely close relationship between the adjacent blocks - ranging from 8 to 11 storeys in height - and the configuration of the neighbourhood.
Each floor is occupied by four apartments of two-bedrooms, with separate kitchen and bathroom.

The structure is based on load-bearing walls and buttresses of red brick which support in situ concrete beams. The roof is a flat concrete slab.
Particular attention has been paid to the bonding of the walls, with the inclusion of special pieces to cover the exposed ends of the concrete beams, fitting together perfectly to form a homogeneous wall which composes the facade of the tower.
The study of the proportions of the windows, along with the provision of special opaque curtains, the use of highly transparent glazing for the accessible windows or the insertion of wall facings of glass blocks reflect the tremendous care with which the architects have controlled the entry of natural light. Thus, the window is conceived of more as an element which is intended to reinforce the close relationship between the interior of the apartments and the natural environment outside than as a mere alteration in the wall in which it appears.

Site plan, typical floor plans and sectioned
axonometric drawing

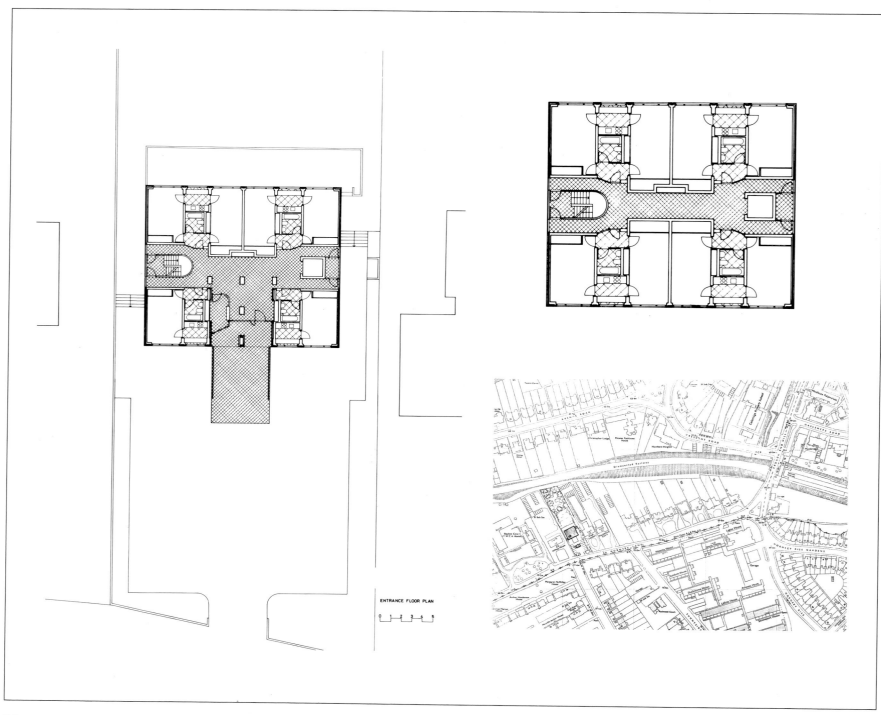

ENTRANCE FLOOR PLAN

0 1 2 3 4 5

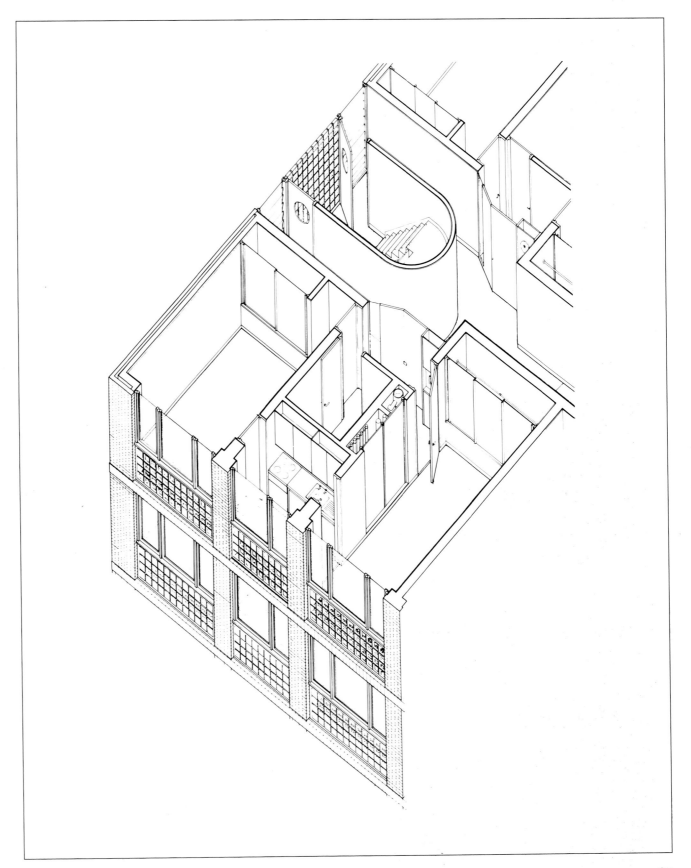

View of the stairs and the exterior of the block

Architect: Gustav Peichl

Hutweidenhof

Scholsstrasse Reinickendorf

1984-1989   Berlin-Tegel (D)

This complex of three blocks united within a single built volume 6 storeys high has been conceived as the closure of a large isolated block situated between three streets and a landscaped area around the Nordgraben in the Reinickendorf district.

This is a building intended for mixed uses, with the ground floor given over to commercial premises and workshops, a sports centre and gym and a cafeteria. The floors above - from the first to the sixth - are occupied by a total of 50 apartments, varying in area from 45 to 110 m2. In addition, the architect has transformed the northern part of the plot into a public park, gathering it all together to form a single recreation area.

The scale of the building, the value given to the public spaces and the relationships established between them are fundamental aspects of the handling of the scheme.
The new construction effectively compacts the lines already formally defined by the existing buildings, at the same time as it suggests formal relationships between the architectural elements and their surroundings which lead to the complex asserting itself as the continuation of the street layout. The plane of the north-facing facade - created by the line which unites the 'prows' of the three blocks constituting a frontal quality that completes the volumes - maintains its interior, domestic character, enjoying as it does views out over the Tegel lake.

The various different schemes reveal how the project evolved towards the discovery of a morphology of its own, declining to compose simple volumes or more primary forms which would take in the whole complex. The Austrian-born Gustav Peichl is one of the few architects to combine a professional career in construction and teaching - as professor at the Vienna Kunstakademie - with journalism - as a cartoonist. In this project as in others in his extensive architectural career, Peichl contributes to the promotion of the revival of housing policy in Berlin, Vienna and the other European cities in which he has built.

Each of his schemes sets out to bring together architecture and nature, combining them in a landscape made serviceable through the conjunction of indepenent built forms.
The subtlety and simplicity of the complex are accompanied by a number of ironic touches. In plan, the buildings can be seen to resemble the structural supports of bridges spanning a river, and the volumes to suggest boats moored to a solid, rigid block-cum-quayside. At the same time, the curving walls and the torqued interiors seek to liberate areas of the dwellings, affording them a certain organic quality.

This building of three towers completes the urban layout here, with Peichl's recent project for the same area in its midst. This other scheme, for a phosphate treatment plant, has very firm links with the Berlin tradition of industrial architecture, binding technical quality and architectonic form closely together. It is worth noting here how a technical installation, a public utility, gives rise to an architectonic unity which is summarised in terms of a smooth, white schematic rationalism.

As on other occasions, in this project G. Peichl has seen to it that his constructions are understood as the final outcome of a process of evolution rather than as an a priori point of departure.

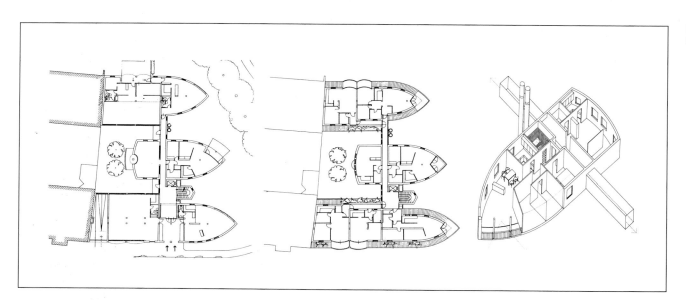

Plans, site location schemes and sectioned
axonometric drawings

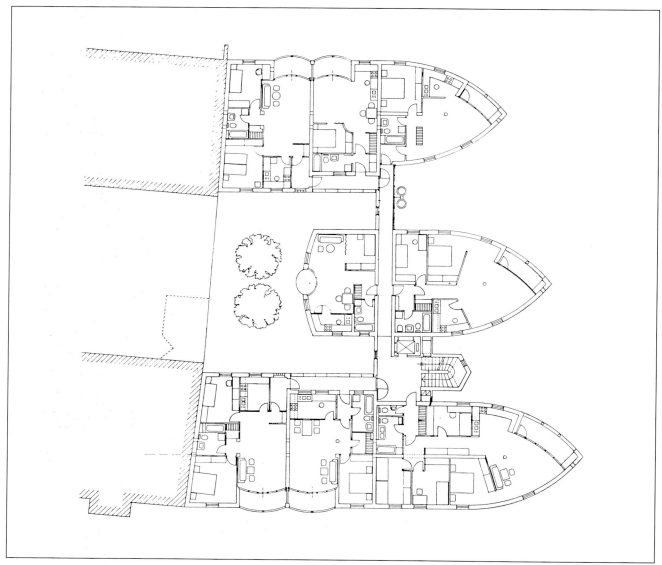

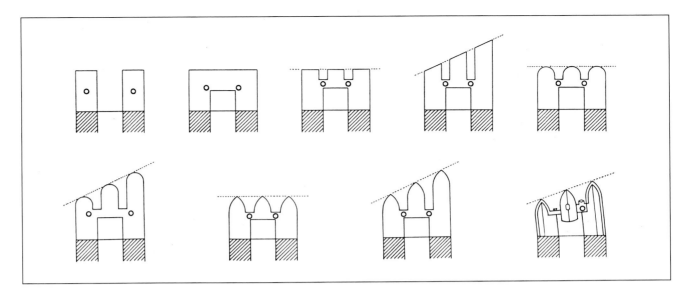

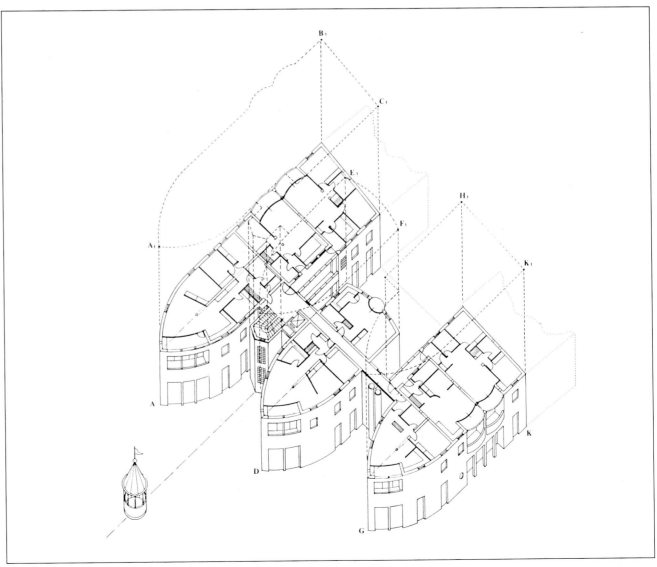

Architects: Esteve Bonell, Josep Maria Gil

Plaça d'Espanya

1981-1984   Sabadell, Barcelona (E)

Occupying the northern half of a square which forms part of the major traffic system surrounding the town, these two public sector apartment blocks complete a new residential district in an industrial town close to Barcelona.

The circular configuration of the Plaça d'Espanya and the considerable buildable depth of the site (14 metres from front to back), together with its great height, are the factors which determined the form and implantation of the building.

With its height of eight storeys, comprising a ground floor given over to commercial premises, with a pedestrian arcade running around the entire building, plus seven floors of apartments, and its expressive character on the urban scale, the complex of two blocks has been ably incorporated into the immense space of the square.

By means of rectilinear planes, the groupings of two apartments to a floor adapt to the curving context of the plaza, achieving an orthogonal form in most of the living areas. Inside the apartments, the living room-dining room area plays a key role in resolving the agreement of the different geometries, given that its situation invites it to define the composition of the whole, modulating the concave plane and seeking to attenuate the linearity and anonymity of the long, tall curving block. In this way, the domestic space is logically resolved, with all of the rooms rectangular, reserving the angular deviation for the largest of the spaces (the living room). The same system is used to emphasise the corners.

Each apartment has two exterior facades, ensuring good illumination and through ventilation.

The appearance of the blocks from the rear, an unalterable convex plane, is modulated by the strips of windows lighting the stair wells. At the same time, at the end of the block, the stair wells serve to resolve the union with the existing urban fabric.

The project's clarity of typology and construction probably constitutes its maximum virtue. The repetition of the same module, based on the adaptation of the geometry to the arc of the perimeter, at the same time resolves the implantation and the volume of the complex with great economy of means.

The material employed - fair-faced brick - undergoes a change in colour on the top two floors in order to crown the blocks, in addition to toning down any excess of height and solidity. At the same time, the balconies have been enlarged to become terraces, with a single circular form, divided by a sheet metal partition, serving a pair of adjoining apartments.

The ground floor accesses serving each of the units are remarkable in the way they adapt to the level of the great plaza by means of steps which raise up the entrance, individually identifying each module through the use of different-coloured ceramic cladding on the facade. In keeping with the homogeneity of the materials used, the simplicity of the composition of the facades and the distribution of the services around the stair well contribute to defining the simple yet effective execution of the scheme.

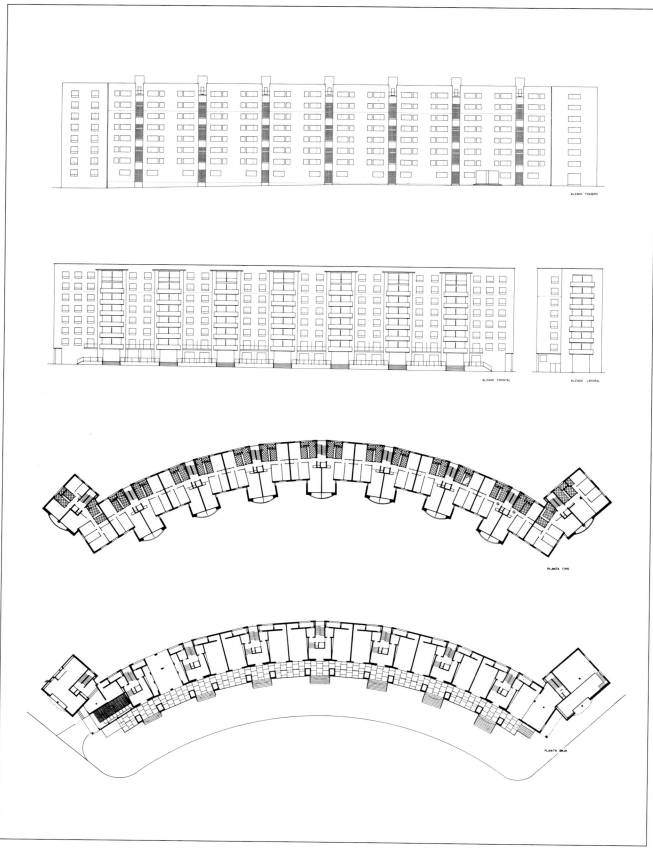

ALZADO TRASERO

ALZADO FRONTAL

ALZADO LATERAL

PLANTA TIPO

PLANTA BAJA

108

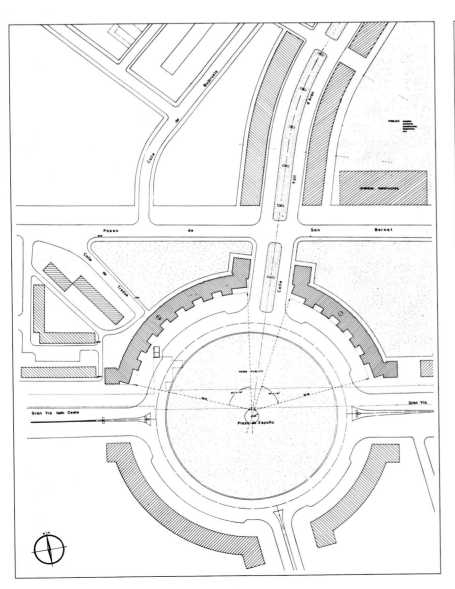

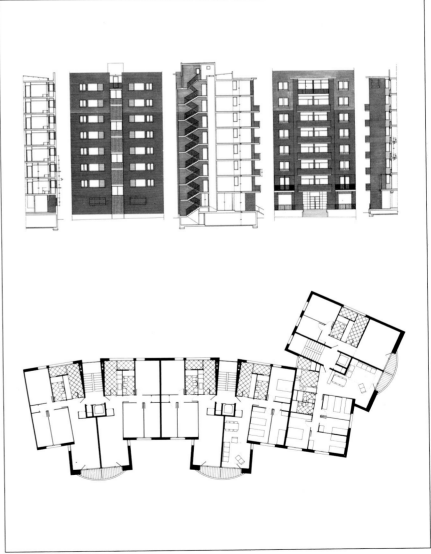

Various views of the exterior

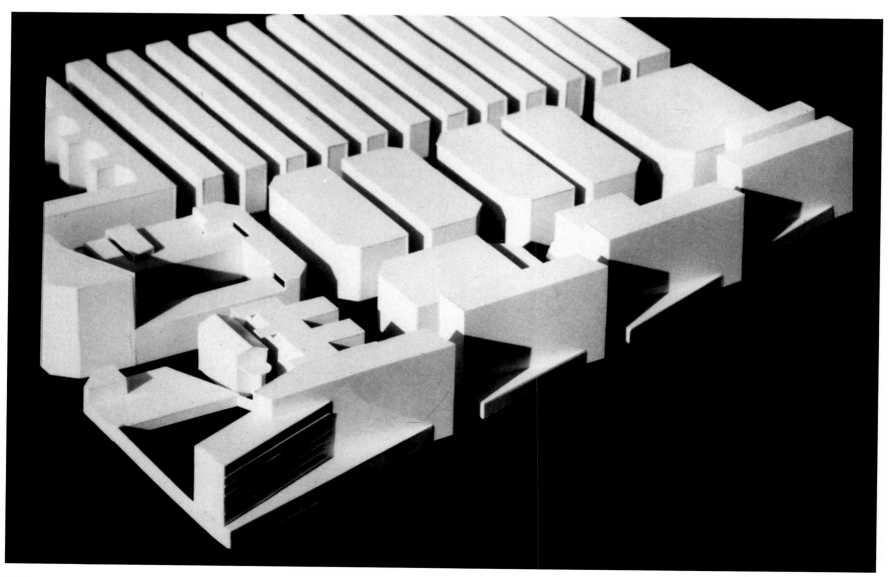

Architect: Joan Pascual Argente

Collaborators: Ramón Ausió, Lluís Badenas, Sonia Blasco
Annanina Kriedler, Xavier Valls, Josep Maria Vivas

Avinguda Icària

1990   Barcelona (E)

This complex of buildings, submitted for the competition for sketch designs for public sector housing, is situated alongside an extensive area of amenities bounded by a wide avenue carrying a high volume of traffic on the edge of the historic centre of Barcelona, in the seafront district of the Barceloneta.

This part of the city, characterised by its peculiar urban morphology, is laid out in linear buildings of considerable height in relation to their scant depth, separated by narrow streets. This building typology impedes the satisfactory functioning of the dwellings and their relationship with the few small public spaces in the vicinity. For this reason, after a study of the planning regulations currently in force here, it was decided not to slavishly follow the alignment marked out by the broad avenue, but to position the main volumes of the new building at right angles to the axis of the existing urban grid. At the same time, the ground floors intended as commercial premises were aligned in accordance with the established urban plan, in order to form a plinth on which to set the seven floors of housing while maintaining the necessary reference to the line of the road.

The project gives priority to the role of these buildings as elements articulating the boundary of one sector of the city, using their siting as a means of organising a qualitative change in the built fabric with the aim of creating a stepped sequence of perspectives along the length of the avenue. In this way the different views of the planned complex are unified, establishing the orderly appearance of the rear sector both at the point of access to the neighbouring seafront district and along the route into the Olympic Village.

The form of the buildings in the first and last blocks has been adapted in keeping with their position as beginning and end of the project, turning the volumetries with the resulting loss of two and one floors, respectively. Thus a more distended facade is created, providing some relief from the proximity of the very dense neighbouring buildings and establishing a clear relation between built mass and occupied volumes.

In accordance with the dimensions determined by the planning regulations as regards the permissible depth of building and the techniques for construction and maintenance, the apartments have been grouped together around central communications nuclei, with a lift and stairs serving the three flats on each floor. Two of these apartments are laid out longitudinally, while the third is perpendicular to the main facade. The interior distribution is directed at optimising the surface area of each apartment, grouping together the sanitary services and eliminating as far as possible any loss of space in corridors or entrance halls. The scheme also allows for the enlarging of certain rooms, such as the bedrooms, by removing the partition walls. To this end, the structural system adopted employs a grid of beams resting on reinforced concrete pillars, walls of fair-faced brick and inverted flat roofs.

The ground floor features the usual commercial premises, facing onto the streets to the west, with garden-courtyards laid out around the accesses to the vestibules. This has allowed the creation of open spaces on a smaller scale, which act as filters between the roadway and the buildings.

The project applies realistic criteria to the interpretation of the existing planning regulations, helping to improve the urban quality of the Barceloneta sector, at present in a state of considerable degradation.

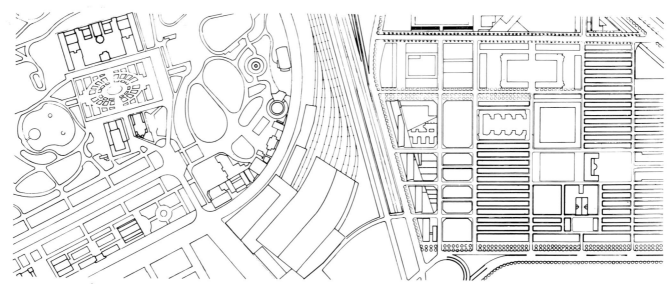

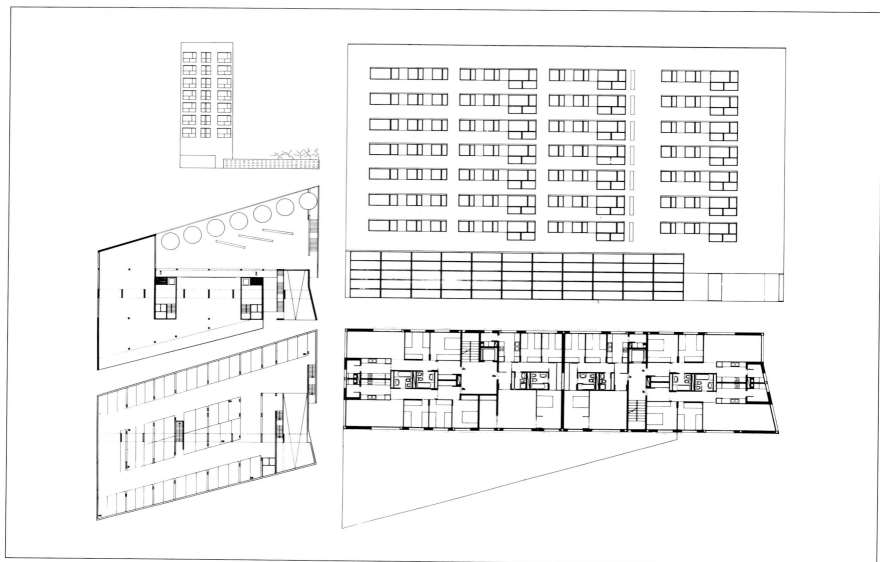

114

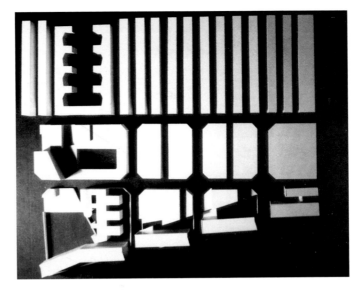

Location plan, site plan, view of the model,
plans, elevations and perspective

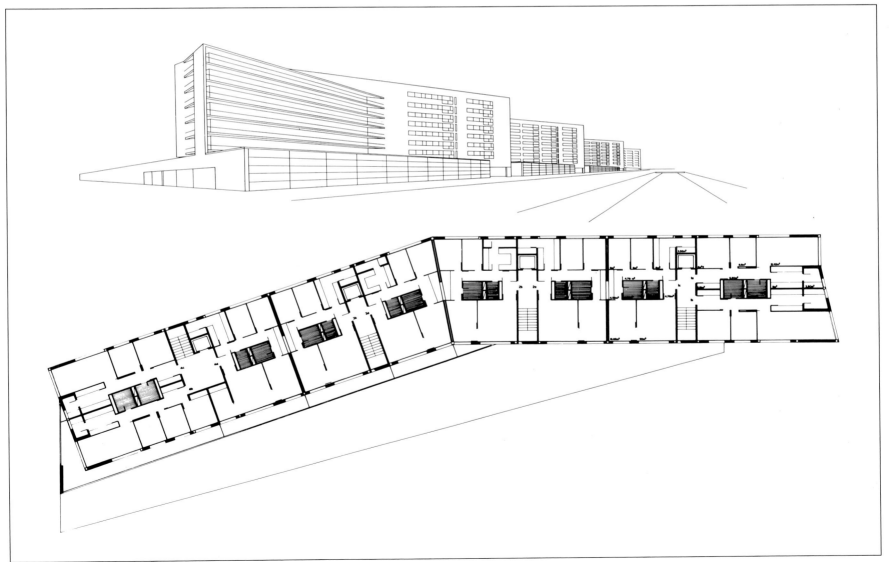

Architect: José Luis Mateo

Collaborators: Antonio Montes, J. Pastor

Catex Poble Nou

C. Bilbao / C. Pallars / Old road to Valencia

1985-1988   Barcelona (E)

Situated in the industrial district of Poble Nou, on the periphery of the historic centre of Barcelona, these 120 subsidised dwellings complete a block partly given over to public amenities, including a cultural centre and a swimming pool, designed by José Luis Mateo.

Poble Nou, its configuration determined by the original fishing village, the old road network - south to Valencia, north to France - and the confrontation with the Cerdà Eixample in the mid-nineteenth century, is still in an uncompleted state, with its vacant lots in the urban fabric and tensions created by the existing buildings and the Cerdà grid to be superimposed on the area.

The building, with its function as privately developed local authority subsidised housing, is conceived on the basis of the logical repetition of an elementary additive unit and its specific contextual distortions at either end. The additive rhythm of the composition can be appreciated in the side facades, underlined by the design of the elements holding railings and balconies in place which, like great masts, serve to unify the projecting volumes of the living room bays.

As the architect explains, the building finds its principal thesis in the turning of its walls, which makes way for various episodes prompted by the uses envisaged and the special circumstances of the context. Thus the chamfered Cerdà corner is configured as an excavated solid, in the same terms as certain architects of the 50s and 60s approached this very problem. The block concludes in a schematic unity in which a number of highly individual elements stand out by virtue of their intrinsic value, such as the wall of the laundry areas which emphasises the movement at the turning of the corner, or the expansion of the oblique partitions enclosing the balconies.

This apartment building completes the intervention begun by the Catex Complex in the same city block, based on the refurbishment of a large factory and the addition of a new volume containing an indoor swimming pool.

It is interesting to note how the aggregation of buildings with nothing in the way of a common characteristic is capable of offering a different approach to urban design, elaborating a series of images which respond to different architectonic tempos.
The residential block undoubtedly provides the opportunity to evaluate the effort to excite interest in a building where the initial conditioning factors called for the strictest realism in its execution.

The conventional construction systems employed, such as the regular grid of reinforced concrete beams or the enclosing walls of fair-faced brick, give a severity to the external appearance which derives dynamic qualities from other elements such as the inclined planes formed by the balconies as they are reduced in size with each move closer to ground level, or the volumes housing the windows on the corner, mentioned above.
Together with the criteria governing the internal distribution, derived from the now obsolete standards formerly applied to the control and construction of public sector housing in Spain, the finishing of the interior vestibules, with their ceilings of wood and marble paving on the floors, seek to apply a more delicate, more mysterious scale to the design of the block.

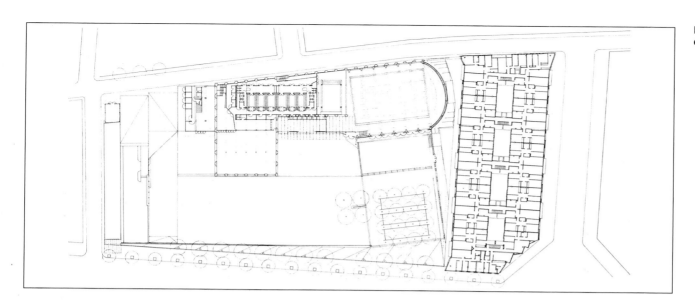

Plan of the complex, typical floor plans and exterios views

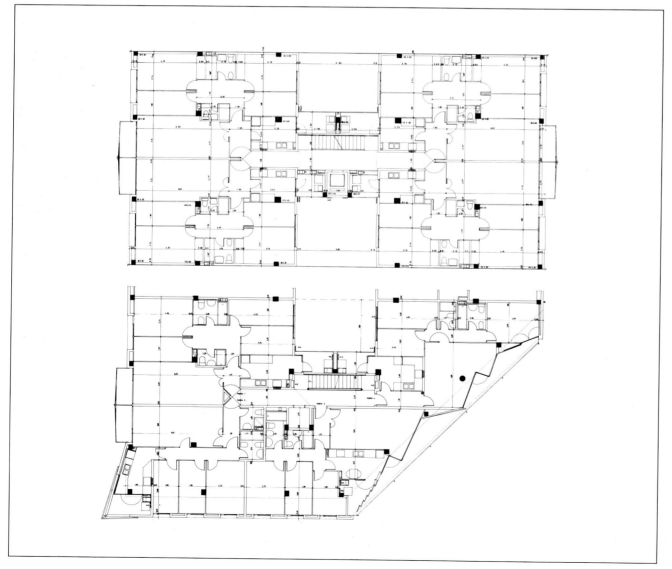

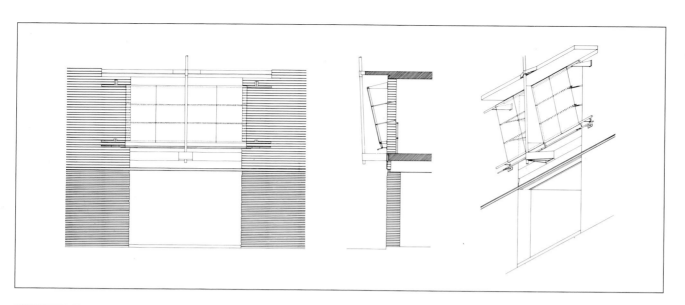

Previous pages: various views of the exterior and of the vestibule of one of the accesses

Partial views and details of the facade

Architects: Hans Kollhoff, T. Dietzsch, Martin Ovaska

Luisenplatz
Charlottenburg

1982-1989   Berlin (D)

Seventy-five public sector apartments, nine attic studios, ten storeys of underground car parking plus three office units are divided between the three blocks which rise up between the buildings dating from Berlin's classical past which have survived until the present day.

The project comes within the terms of the IBA, Berlin's International Architecture Exhibition, the aim of which is to revive the - until lately neglected - work of treating the street as a system of urban spaces, prompting the use of materials deeply rooted in the history of construction in Germany. The project, the winner of the 1982 competition, comprises seventy-five apartments, in two-, three- and four-bedroom units, built to a height in line with that of the neighbouring buildings - Charlottenburg castle, with its park and pavilion by Schinkel, and a series of bourgeois apartment houses along the bank of the river Spree.

The curving wall which defines the scheme submitted for the competition is in continuity with the proposal established by Schinkel's pavilion, built in 1824, in its orthogonal relationship with the street axes. The second block exploits its cross-shaped plan by means of the composition of volumes opposite the Schloss Garten.

During the first stage of the planning process, a house dating from the end of the last century, which had originally been earmarked for demolition, was integrated into the project, with a complex overlaying of the new curve onto the wall of the old building. The compactness of the three blocks is maintained by the transparent curtain wall, which does not enclose a single arris of the building, and the potent form of the eaves of the roof, while the cubic volume of the old house is emphasised by having it project forward from the established alignment.

The use of cubic forms, endlessly compartmentalised, with a labyrinth of narrow stairways, which has been traditional for residential buildings in Berlin since the last century, is not only accepted here, but adopted as a conceptual reference point in the design of the project.

The perimeter of the curving block should, as originally planned, have been completed, but the process of political decision-making and planning considerations resulted in a break in the glazed curve, excluding the possibility of seamlessly interweaving the new buildings into the existing fabric.
The blocks are responsive to the passage of the river Spree - the source of the unfavourable soil conditions which made it necessary for part of the building to be constructed on foundation piles sunk to a depth of more than twelve metres - and to the visual attractions of their setting, with the long block facing the baroque castle of Charlottenburg. All of these factors are brought to bear in the staging of this grand urban scene, where the enormous wing of the roof, the great glazed gallery-window and the industrial brick contrast with the picturesque coloration of the neighbouring buildings.
An exterior glazed area functions as an insulation system and a porch running round the entire project. The roof imposes itself as the vertebral element with regard to its surroundings, as well as charging the whole with its assymetrical dynamism and lightening the solidity of the buildings in their setting.

This project betrays a nostalgic attitude to the traditional city, reacting against the massive housing schemes which were built in the late sixties. The building here combines its character as closing segment in the city block and urban element, being perceived as a linear container, relating plan and elevation by means of form and construction.

The building is constructed with load-bearing walls whose engineering bricks were made with a blue industrial clinker, and have an almost square exposed face.

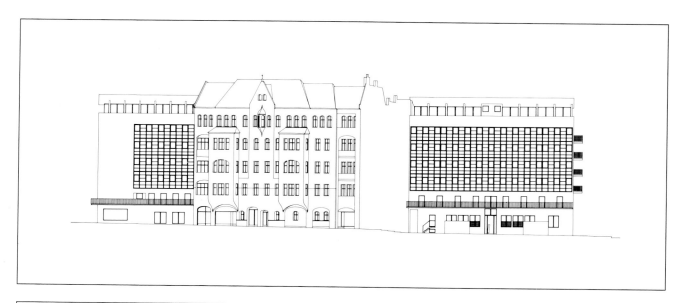

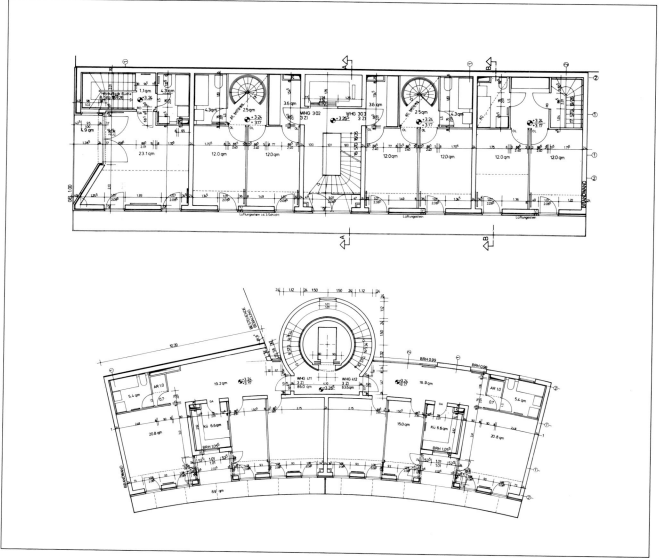

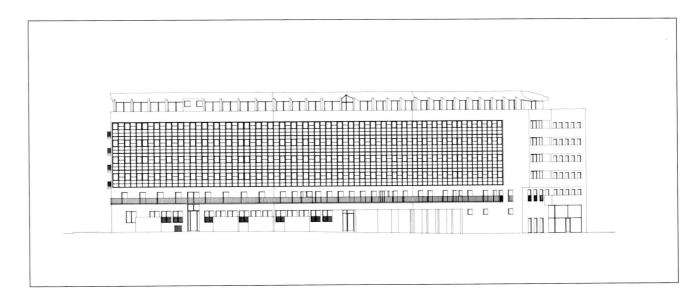

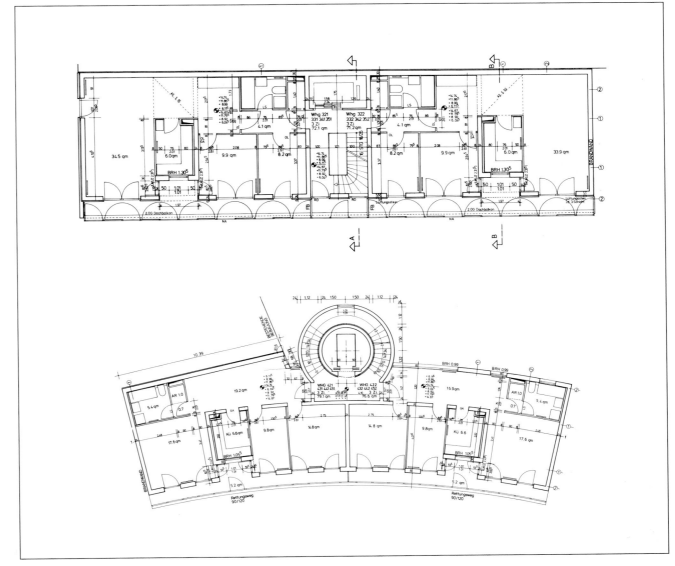

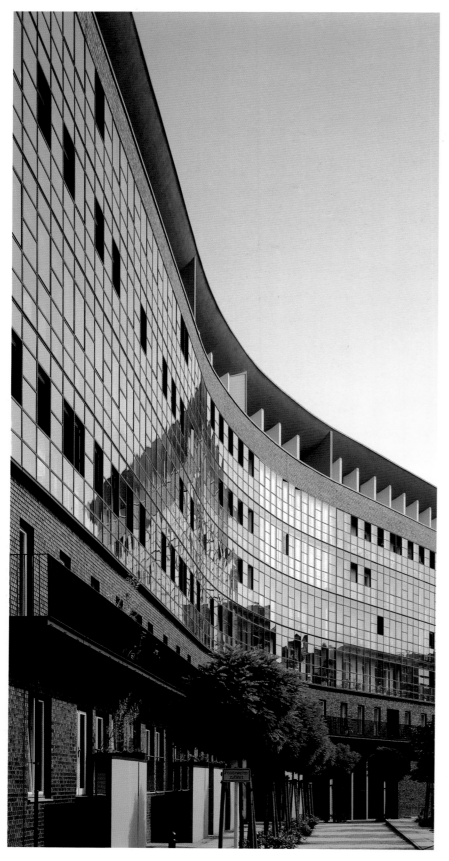

Various views of the exterior and general perspective of the block

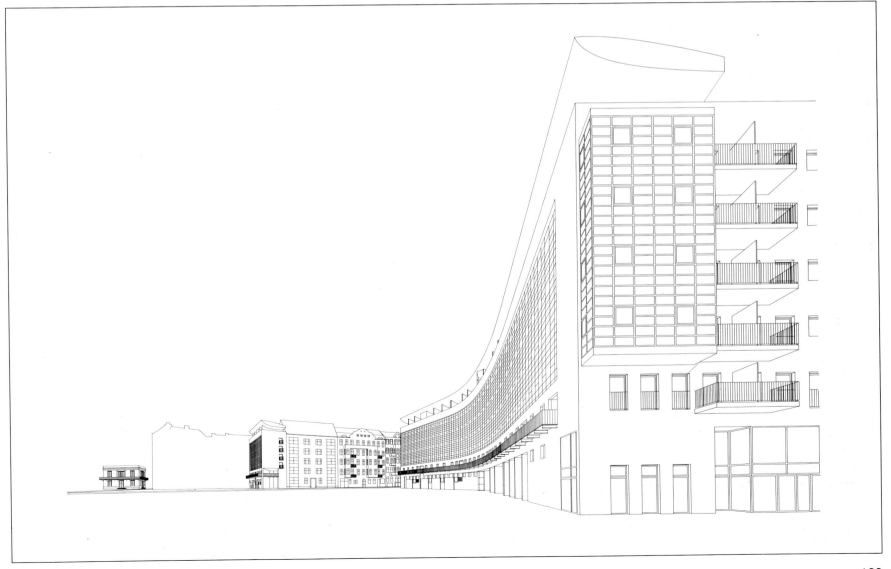

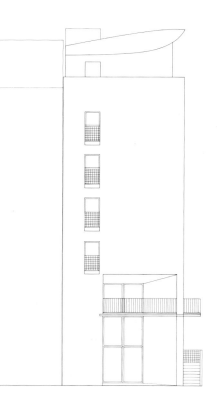

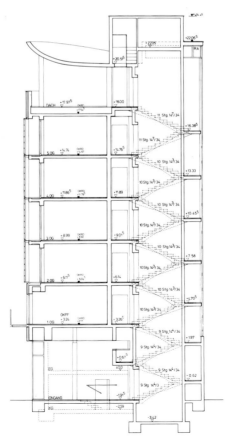

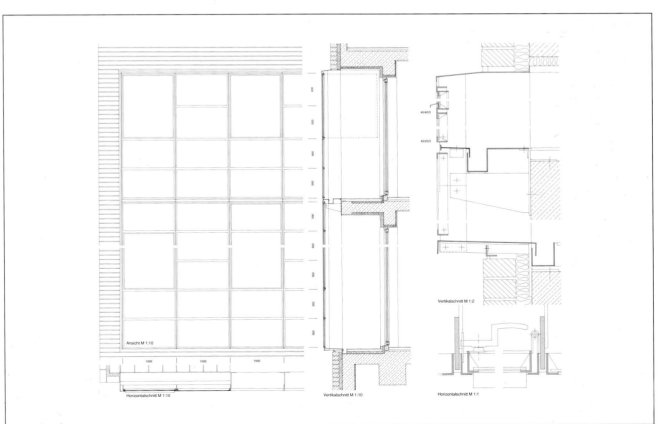

Ansicht M 1:10

Horizontalschnitt M 1:10

Vertikalschnitt M 1:10

Vertikalschnitt M 1:2

Horizontalschnitt M 1:1

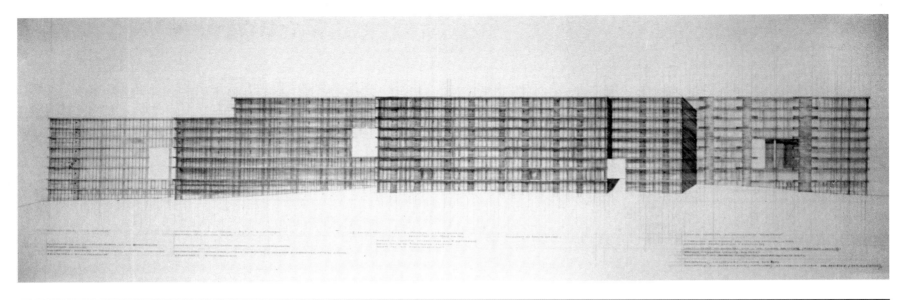

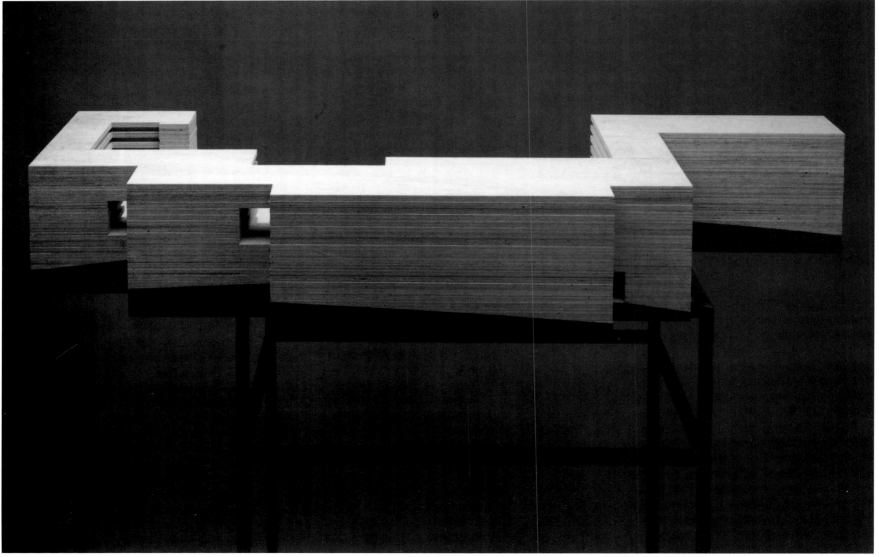

Architects: Herzog & de Meuron

Collaborator: Dieter Gysin

Schwarz Park
Gellerstrasse

1988   Basle (CH)

The building stands in a large wooded park on the edge of the historic 19th century nucleus of Basle. The topography is characterised by the presence of a plateau bordered by a water-meadow by the side of the river.

The project came first in the competition held in the city in 1988; it is currently at the design stage. The urban design concept is developed in terms of the concentration of the mass of the building along the street axis, without encroaching on the existing layout of the park.

The scheme has its origins in certain acute reflections on place and form, neither determining them from the outside nor fixing them in advance, as might occur in a simpler fashion in a classical building. In this case the internal structure of the building determines the section, the floor plans and the facades. The projecting volume of this massive form communicates the geometry of its boundary beyond the park, as far as the water-meadow. Its silhouette is largely intelligible in terms of the relationship between its proportions and those of the imposing neighbouring volume of the Bethesda hospital.

A compact module of dwellings acts as a unit of repetition, composing the dimensions of the block as this advances longitudinally while at the same time changing the materials.
In the light wells and stair wells, reinforced concrete is used, with refractory brick for the chimneys, and tinted concrete for the column-like exterior towers.

All of the vertical elements have a structural function, at the same time as they discharge a specific function of their own. The space created between the towers, open to various different uses, becomes the negative form in opposition to the potency of the vertical elements.
If the city plan of Basle allows us to distinguish between the compact geometrical forms which compose the centre, and other softer zones which characterise the periphery, this project belongs to the intermediary areas, those still in an undefined condition, occupying a site on the borderline.

For Jacques Herzog and Pierre de Meuron, the personal detail, the identification of each intervention, is anachronistic. The abstraction of the materials and the intelligent formalisation of facades and masses mean that, in their projects, it is essential to pay particular attention to that which is given formal shape in the labours of each of the people at work on the construction. Their constructive rationalism evokes certain images, not figurative, but the product of a logic created by the indissoluble unity between space and constructive idea.
A large part of the interest of this project lies in the way it is sited, the way it closes off spaces which are its own yet public, generated by large-scale elements with identical yet displaced geometries and plane forms, twisted throughout their vertical extension. The large openings, which transcend definition as mere doors or windows, create a permeability between park and building, between living space and recreation space, between the opaque built wall and the natural transparencies of the glazing. The building configured in this way is comparable to some agglomerate material in which each one of the constituent elements retains its individual character in the final compound.

Thus, in the plan, the block gives form to an examination of how the presence of the surrounding context and the building interchange links of relationship, effectively arresting the process of decomposition experienced by many Swiss cities after the end of the Second World War.

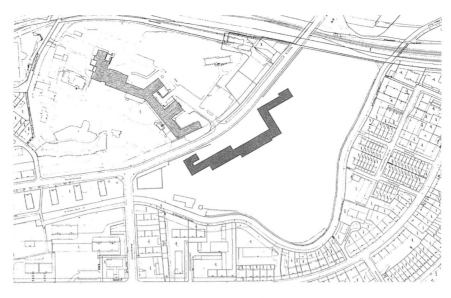

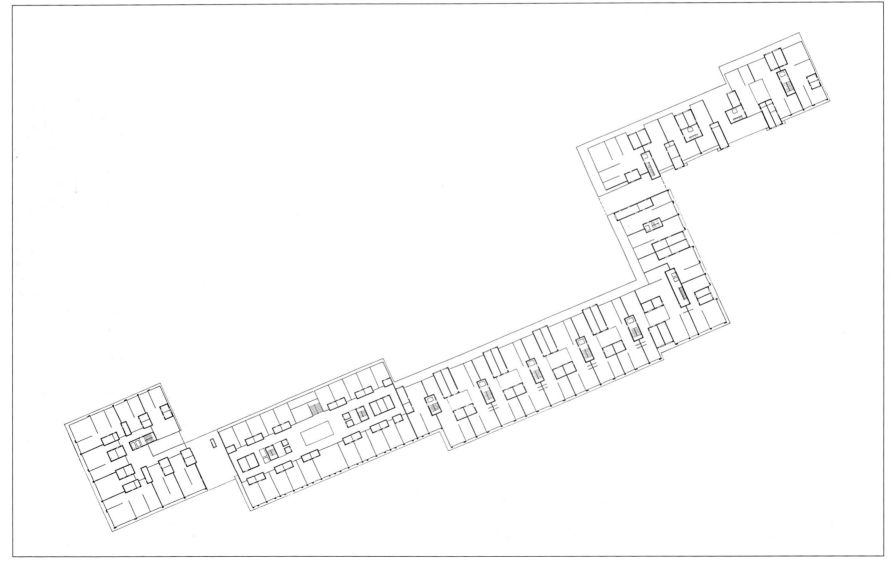

Site plan, typical floor plan and view of the model

Architect: Francesco Venezia

Collaborators: Paolo di Caterina, Rosaria Gargiulo,
Riccardo Lopes, Andrea Cosenza, Luis Pereira, Paula Pinheiro

Piazza a San Pietro a Patierno

1988-1990   Naples (I)

The former village of San Pietro in Patierno, which the recent expansion of the city's suburbs has swallowed up and pressed against the boundary of the Capodichino airport, is the location for this urban recovery scheme. The project assumes a residual approach which takes in the new Piazza Centrale, the offices of the electoral district, police headquarters and a complex of 60 apartments.
This programme was formulated in the aftermath of a major, and tragic, earthquake which Naples suffered in November 1980. The alarming problems affecting the city were thrown into relief: environmental degradation, chronic shortages of housing, services and public amenities and the uneven and unbalancing congestion between the historic centre and the outlying suburbs.

The Extraordinary Reconstruction Programme set in motion by the Italian government establishes the criteria of intervention and the corresponding supervision and steering procedures to be carried out on the architectural projects. This operation specifically marks the move from a culture of expansion to one of transformation, setting up a critical reflection on the possibilities for intervention in and upgrading of the peripheral areas of the city.

This scheme is situated in the most significant of the surviving fragments, and takes concrete form in a project which is at once restoration, restructuring and new building. This provides an opportunity to initiate a complex operation of urban recovery, based not simply on satisfying the need for housing but also the general upgrading of the quality of the urban environment, in this case closely linked to the form of the existing layout, by means of particularised interventions in the most rundown areas. In this way the zone is given an architectural unity, consisting in part of existing buildings, in part of buildings transformed through refurbishment and demolition, and in part of new buildings on vacant sites, whose constituent elements have been defined on the basis of their own specific urban role.

The central concern of the project has been to make an urban refurbishment operation compatible with the new public function assigned to the complex. This has meant overcoming the contradiction generated by the criteria relating the building to its context and the proportions of the unit of repetition in the built fabric on the one hand, and the norms which, governing the new standards, set up relationships at odds with the traditional standards, on the other.

Project decisions here followed an analogous approach to intervention in both the existing and the new additions. The object has been to transcend the distinction between restoration, urban restructuring and new building through the use, in the latter, of traditional connecting and mediating elements in order to relate the domestic and the human scale.

The old buildings have been put to the service of the new programme, transforming them and changing their functional role. In parallel with this, for the new constructions, an urban type - that of the block with a main volume and other adjacent secondary volumes - has been chosen with the aim of allowing the form of the building to be undifferentiated with regard to the functions it accomodates and to enjoy complete correspondence with its particular urban role.

This complex project has been handled by the Neapolitan architect with discipline, applying rules which have given him the necessary compositional freedom, transcending the example of the historical context and the site and taking special care over the building's proportions and articulations.
The continuous dialogue with the natural and artificial features of the southern Italian landscape is affirmed in an architecture understood as a constructed action, committed to fostering constant poetical study.
In Francesco Venezia's work there is a predominant use of materials which demonstrate his tactile perception, free of finishes which might simulate other origins or textures. Each one of the component parts of the building works by subtraction or addition, in order thus to rediscover or to transfer the meaning of its use to the space itself.

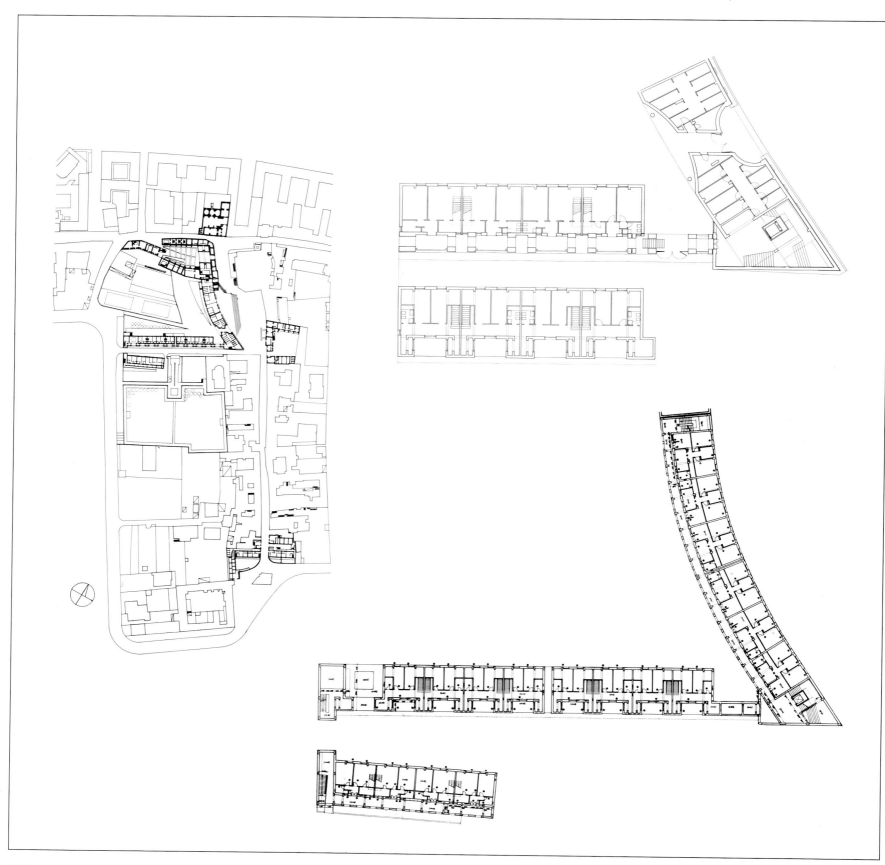

138

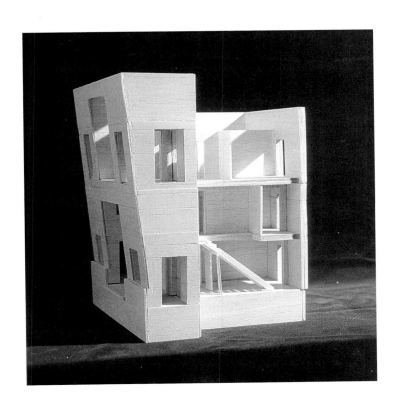

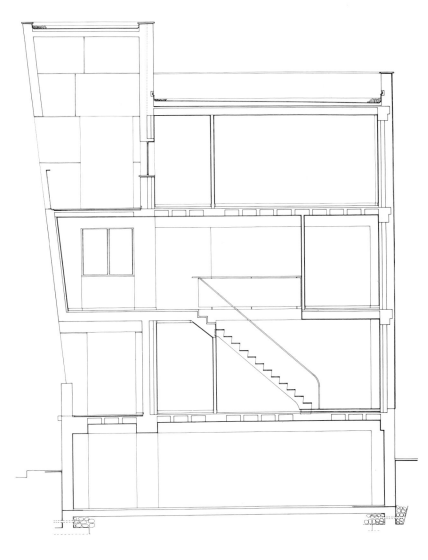

Architect: Francisco Javier Sáenz de Oíza

Site supervision: Félix González Vela,
Javier Sáenz Guerra

Polígono 38, La Paz
Avenida Doctor Tapia / M-30

1986-1990   Madrid (E)

In 1986, the Consejería de Ordenación del Territorio, the planning authority of the Comunidad de Madrid, decided to invite a group of six Spanish architects to study a site adjacent to the M-30 motorway, the development of which was determined in the Plan General for Madrid as an exact helicoid.
Under the name 'Architecture as solution', synonymous with the objective of the competition, Oíza's scheme for this longitudinal building was the one selected.
While the other proposals set out to fragment the complex to be built into smaller blocks, Oíza exaggerated the dimensions of his construction, minimising the windows and inviting awareness of its monumental proportions.

The building-cum-wall conforms in general terms to the regulations strictly governing the urban layout, occupying a decontextualised site surrounded by asphalt, putting forward a singular, introverted scheme which closes in on itself as protection from the exterior.

Standing to the west of the historic centre of Madrid, alongside the M-30 motorway, this 600 metre-long block, situated within a residential estate beside a major traffic junction, occupies a plot with an irregular form, raised 10 metres above the level of the motorway, a circumstance which made it necessary to rectify the north-west boundary of the plot to build a new lateral road affording direct communication.

The block curves in a spiral with its origin at the geometrical centre, closing around itself to exclude the acoustic and visual contamination created by an eight-lane motorway.
The project reveals how a personal approach can resolve the urban problems caused by the application of obsolete planning regulations, refusing to be disconcerted by the risk involved in monumentalising residential architecture. The subject of heated polemic, this project defends its architect's personal vision of the city's periphery.
Two thousand windows protect the block from the heavy traffic at the same time as they order the skin of the elliptical facade, while the

changes in height of the stepped building respond to urban conditions and the number of apartments in each residential nucleus. The height alternating between four and eight storeys, the majority of the apartments are duplex, housing families displaced by large-scale building works in other similar residential estates in Madrid.

The complex comprises 346 apartments, divided into programmes of two-, three- and four-bedroom units. The two-bedroom dwellings are laid out on a single level.
The total number of dwellings increases at a uniform rate throughout the length of the block, amounting to 48 units with two apartments to a floor. These units are divided in turn into two typologies, according to whether they belong to the the generating curve or the rectilinear stretch of the block.

The programme of complementary services for the complex consists of a social and comunity centre for the residents and a series of small shops on the ground floor.

The facade overlooking the M-30, of red brick, is hatched by the little windows ordered in rows, while the radically different inner facade is painted with a surprising, colourist design, repeated in phase with the sequence of double terraces of the duplex apartments.

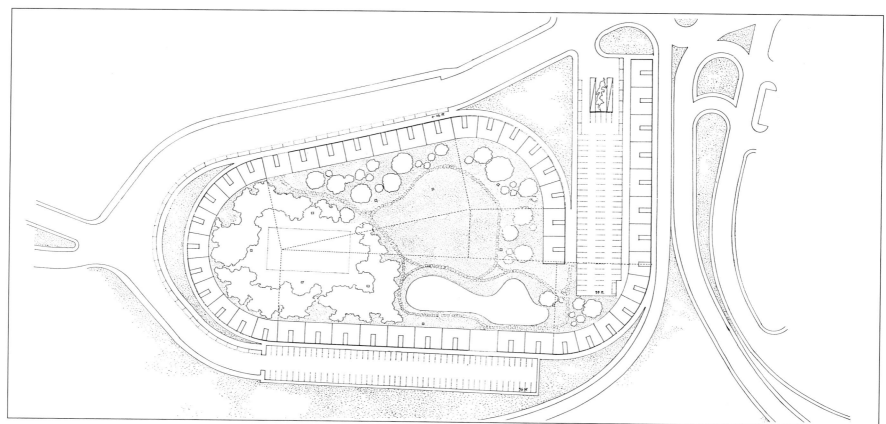

Site plan, view of the exterior and typical floor plans

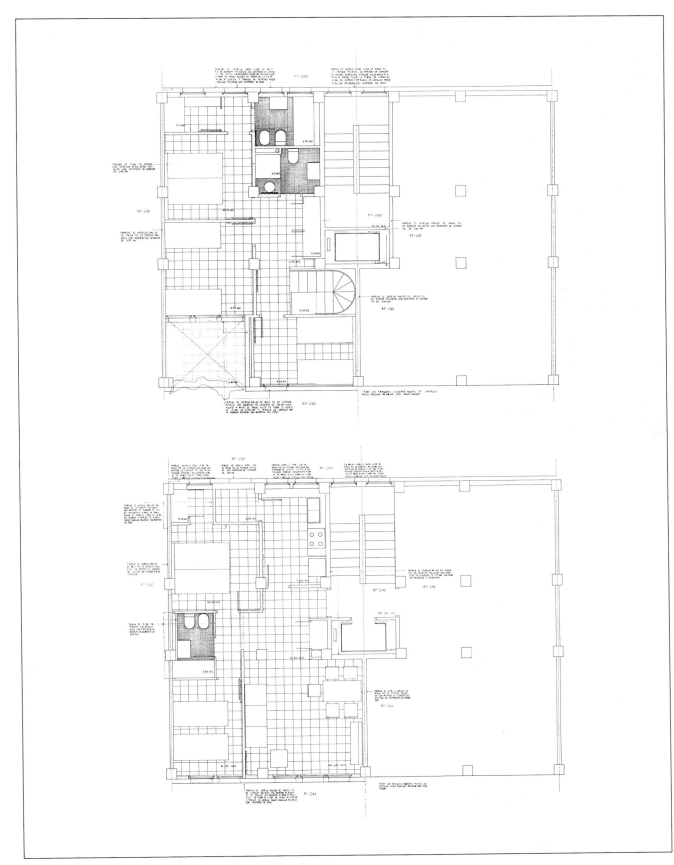

Following pages: elevation and various view of the exterior

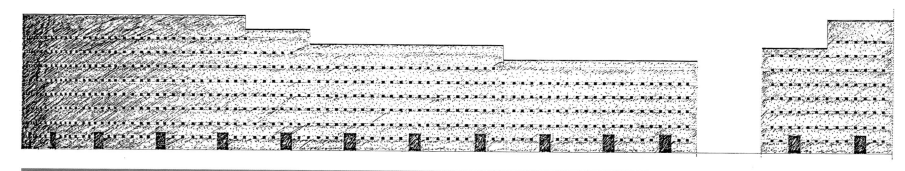

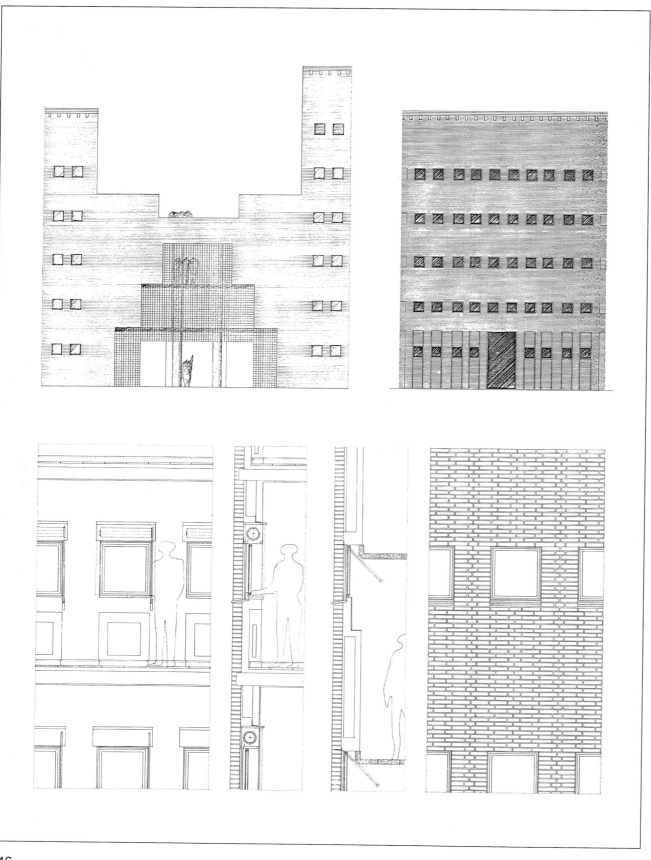

Details of the building and view of the large internal courtyard from the pergola

146

Architects: Atsushi Kitagawara + ILCD Inc

Cloudy-Spoon

1987-1988   Hoya, Tokyo (J)

The starting point for the project is a plot of irregular dimensions in the chaotic setting of the Hoya district. The building, with its double-trapezoid form, consists of ground floor, five identical floors of small individual apartments, and an attic studio.
The initial premises set out to give a literal conception of what it means to live in a block with a double facade (made necessary by the presence of a busy motorway) to the building's appearance, through the creation of a light, almost invisible skin which conforms a void space extending the full height of the building.

Kitagawara's interest in the metropolis, in the shadows cast by the city's empty spaces, in the solitude created by traffic congestion, the buildings with their backs turned to the street or the skyscraper office blocks against the black night sky, divides into two extremes: its demands and its conveniences.
For this Japanese architect, the realistic vision of the city is no longer that provided by a book, a window or a walf through the streets, but the one transmitted by the electronic images of cinema or TV screens. The city is in disorderly flight towards mechanisms of self-expression which reveal it as an excessive compilation of living ruins, together forming a labyrinth. His architecture seeks nothing other than to be a part of the metropolis, an accumulation of interior cities, in need of time to form itself as space.

Kitagawara belongs to a generation of young architects who regard their cities as chaotic sprawls, and whose response is a colourist architecture turned outwards towards this reality, standing apart from the spartan, minimalist aesthetic of the Japanese tradition, favouring instead a more active, more visceral imagery, and taking refuge in a surrealist irony.
These architects believe in buildings as generic, commercial objects, composed of materials which provoke images that are incongruous, obscure, almost sinister. What is important is not the coherence in a piece of work, but the independence with which it is undertaken.
As a representative of the 'New Architecture', Kitagawara has created an urban entity with this building, which represents his way of thinking.

As the architect himself observes, the basic premise is the creation of the visible, and although architecture has always been regarded as a bridge which takes us from here to there, with no return, the question is where to suspend this bridge.

The building is transformed into a virtual box, which contains within the hope of unreservedly pleasing its users.
The apartments are laid out around a vertical communications core which gives onto a corridor, exposed to the elements, that distributes and provides access to the dwellings. As the width of the trapezoidal block increases, so too does the surface area of the rooms in the apartments; nevertheless, these are always based on minimum dimensions with a limit of 20 to 25 m2.
In contrast to the restricted surface area of the plan, the apartments have been designed with a height of 4 metres - the maximum permitted - to create a vertical space which, not without irony, makes it possible to include an intermediate level even in the toilet.
In this way, the apartments are generally divided into a living room which communicates with the room containing the tatamis, with the option of opening up completely to convert the whole apartment into a single space.

An open metal structure orders the exterior of the complex, as if waiting to be filled up at any moment with new living units. The building's structure is of reinforced concrete with a steel grid.

In all of this, the architecture as constructed exemplifies an observation made by the architect: everything is a beautiful deception.

Various views of the exterior and of the model

Various views of the exterior and of the two blocks

Architects: Erkki Kairamo, Kristian Gullichsen, Timo Vormala

Collaborators: Aulikki Jylhä, Juhani Kauppinen, Pekka Nieminen, Marita Nylen, J. Maunula

Asunto-Oy Hiiralankaari

1982-1983   Westend, Espoo (SF)

Situated in a densely built-up suburb, with linear blocks up to four storeys high, the complex is nonetheless surrounded by a rural setting.

As with the majority of recent buildings in this zone, the construction system employed is based on precast concrete panels, framed in steel. While the seaward facade is dominated by a system of balconies which extends over the structure of prefabricated units, the rear facade is organised on the basis of private courtyards, formally resolved through the simultaneous interplay of the horizontal lines created by the sliding windows and the vertical lines of the stairways.

Erkki Kairamo, together with Kristian Gullichsen and Timo Vormala, the other Finnish architects with whom he has shared a professional studio since 1973, makes disciplined use of the elements which constitute the modern architectural tradition of his country. The three jointly share the responsibilities of each commission, although the personality of the main designer is unequivocally reflected in the finished work.

Within the framework of a cultural context traditionally receptive to the formal and technical innovations of the twenties and thirties, this team of architects reworks a modern vocabulary which culminates in an exposition that is logical, intelligently adapted to the programme, and sensitive to the manner in which it relates to the surrounding landscape. The city's planning regulations conditioned the volume and silhouette of the block, with the result that the residents' car park and recreation areas were moved to the rear facade behind the courtyards, although there is also a public car park in front of the building.

The formal juxtaposition of the module composed by the stair well and the terrace with its exposed structure sets up an alternating rhythm that runs the length of the block, counterpointing void and solid, giving each section of the facade its individual character.

The precast concrete panels (mostly clad with white ceramic tiles, with large green pieces on the ground floor and in the stair well) articulate the facades; however, to achieve greater structural and formal lightness and independence, in contrast to the rigidity of the block, counterpoint is offered by the groups of balconies constructed of in situ concrete.

The glazed wall, set in the context of the concrete grid of the facade, advances and recedes, creating a spatial disposition which allows the construction of courtyards in direct contact with the apartments, letting views of the woodland filter through to the interior of the building. The long exterior facade maintains the line of the flat roof, tracing the inflections of the wall.

The structure, rationalised by an orthogonal scheme, is based on pillars and beams which formalise the block geometrically and optimise the services and facilities with which the complex is provided.

156

Various views of the exterior

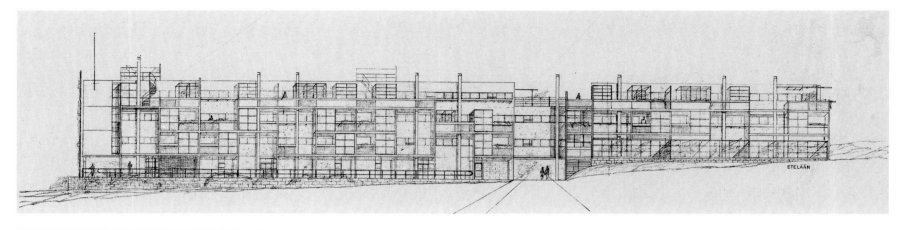

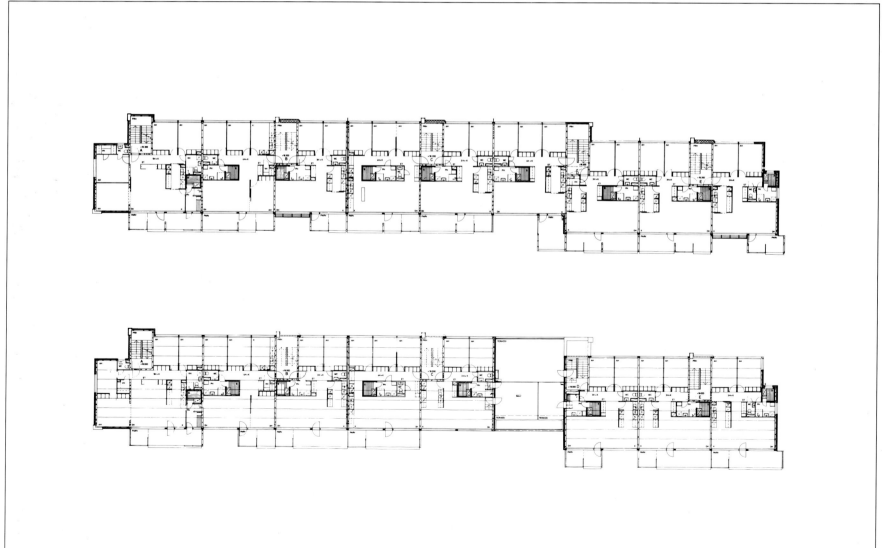

Architect: Shin Takamatsu

Cube II-III

1986-1987   Amagasaki, Hyogo (J)

This little apartment block has been constructed in a city characterised by its past brilliance and a profoundly pervasive blend of traditional landscape and the progressive spirit, in the disorderly setting of the Amagasaki district.
This project is one of a series of property developments in the city of Hyogo, each one of which reveals significant new discoveries and innovative solutions.

The familiarity of the programme - the block is another complex of apartments for single people, and thanks to the strict conditions governing its development did not differ in cost or surface area from the first scheme submitted - caused the architect's interest to be centred on the treatment of the surfaces of the facade, such as the balconies, and the design of the spacious entrance zone, while this concentration can be gauged in the quality of the materials used to keep down the cost of the finishing and detailing.

The design of the communal spaces was determined by the desire to give maximum expressiveness to the facade, which divides the apartment block into two parts: one acting as a socle, reinforcing the base of the building - composed of a regular grid pattern of columns - and the other, above the first, taking the form of a cross which contains the apartments on the top two floors. The delicate hierarchy, in terms of scale, presented by the transparent and opaque enclosures of the balconies generates a facade separated into the apartment block and its roof, a roof which, by means of semi-circular concrete pillars, gives vertical individuality to each of the apartments, in reference to the architect's fascination with night and the half moon.

The apartments are organised on the basis of a construction system which has no formal relationship with the exterior. The repetition of axes, partition elements, and the architect's own personal symbolism make the building the expression of a solitary vision of the city.

As Takamatsu himself concedes, there are few residential buildings in which the apartments are as small as they are here.

This five-storey building, set off the ground on a raised base, has been constructed with a structure of reinforced concrete, pillars and metal ties.

Shin Takamatsu defines himself as an architect who creates shadows and submerged, dark spaces. He prefers not to use natural daylight, and opts instead for settings that are nocturnal and urban. For him, the city is not the product of physical forms and social organisation, but is structured by its own visions, assembled from its dense, intense images. It should be noted that Takamatsu's vision of the city clearly reflects the conditions of the urban environment, and his buildings are conceived as almost exaggerated responses to this establishing of contextual relationships. That is not to say, of course, that his constructions adapt to their setting, but rather, on occasion, adopt an aggressive stance towards the city that envelops them.

Nevertheless, Takamatsu's position, rich in ideas and suggestions, situates him within a generation with a latently innovative approach to construction, influenced by Gilles Deleuze' and Félix Guattari's theories of simulacra and experiment:
'... There are two different ways of doing things. They are each completely different in character, but they should both be complementary. One of the processes pushes you into a fantasy relationship with the object. When fantasy is engaged to an excessive degree, the sense of scale is restricted and this makes the object a non-architectural entity. The second creative process is based on the almost paranoid observation of the operations of correspondence produced between the two scales. ...'

Perhaps for this Japanese architect, creativity is subject to the excessive flow of fantasy and his struggle to combat this excess.

Plans, section and partial view of the
facade

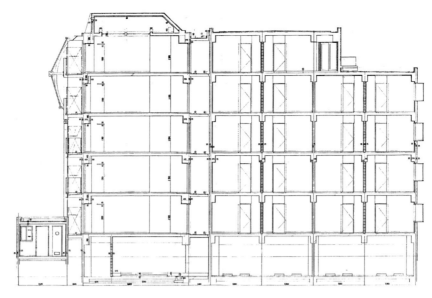

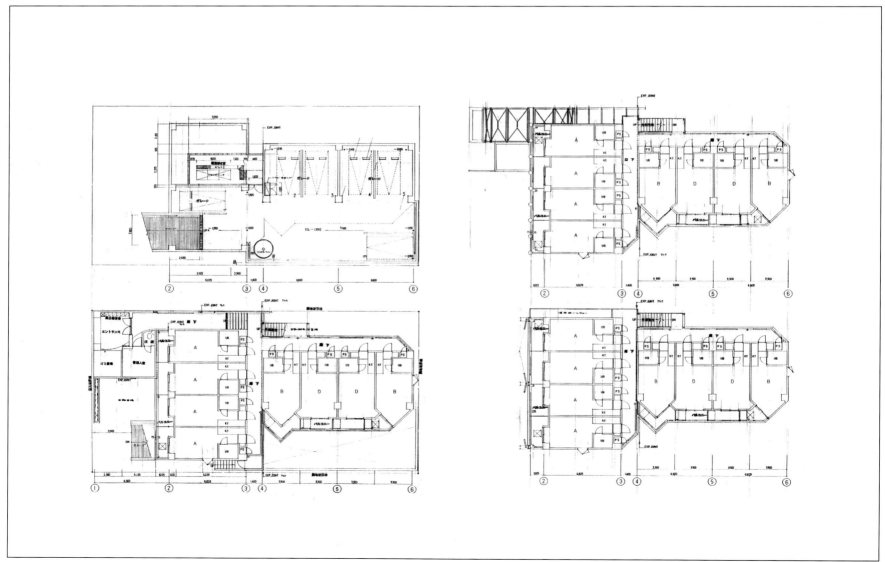

163

Architects: Nicholas Grimshaw & Partners,
Sally Draper, Mark Fisher, Rowena Fuller

Grand Union Walk

Camden Town

1986-1988   London (GB)

Following on the demolition of a large factory building, formerly an industrial bakery, in Camden Town, there was a need to restructure the resulting urban void, by no means ideally suited for residential use.
The site is defined to the east by Camden High Street, and to the west by a major road to Kentish Town, one of the enormous, heavily used radial traffic routes on the outskirts of central London. To the south, the housing comes up against Camden Road, with its busy traffic intersection, while to the north it is bounded by the Grand Union canal which cuts longitudinally across the district.
Camden Council approved the construction of a residential development alongside a large supermarket, although the exact positioning of the complex was left to the architect to decide. After an exhaustive study of the movements of the heavy lorries loading and unloading in the bays at the rear of the supermarket's storage area, an adjoining strip of land with planning approval was proposed, 10 metres wide and running parallel to the canal.

The scheme chose to reject the apparently more advantageous southward orientation of the housing (promising substantial benefits in terms of heat and light) because of the levels of pollution, both acoustic and atmospheric, produced by the heavy vehicles serving the large supermarket adjacent to the apartment block. This decision took material form in the avoidance of any opening in the south facade, to shut out the noise of the lorries manoeuvring.

The apartments open, instead, onto an attractive view of the canal bank with its leafy vegetation, reinforcing this contact - which seemed initially inconceivable - by means of a highly sophisticated automatic opening mechanism on the large glass door giving onto the balcony, which is lifted up to disappear from sight. At the same time, a system of protection and separation was constructed along the boundary with the canal, as well as allowing pedestrian passage underneath the building and providing parking spaces for the residents' cars.

The intervention takes the form of a row of ten two-storey housing blocks with three apartments to a floor, plus a maisonette and a studio

apartment. These last two are situated above the control gate which gives access to a private passage serving the houses.

The distribution of the dwellings derives from the negative conditions which their location gives rise to, with a special concern for letting daylight into those interior zones of the house with no direct opening to the south.
The open, L-shaped plan allows the bedroom in the double space to face the large door-cum-window with its industrial vertical-opening system. This automatic mechanism makes it possible for the double-height dining room to act as an external space, with the disappearance of the great glass door giving onto the canal in the summer months.
The privacy of the interior of the apartments is ensured by the system of electronically controlled aluminium slats on the exterior which can be raised or lowered independently of the doors they screen.

The materials employed in the construction of the entire structure and the exterior finishes are mostly of industrial origin: high-density concrete blocks, precast concrete sole plates and roofs with a gradient of only 10 degrees, composed of aluminium panels with an inner lining of felt.
The double-wall facade, using the British system of rain screen cladding, has been constructed of very slender overlapping aluminium panels (3 millimetres thick), protected by a surface treatment of polymer resin. This method creates an air cavity between the panels and the inner wall, preventing water and damp from the canal reaching the interior of the apartments.

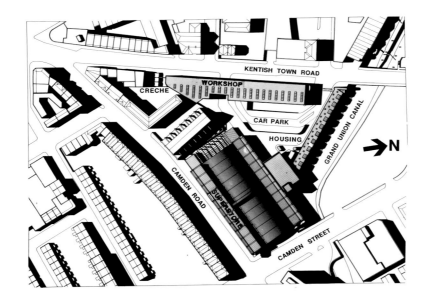

Site plan and various views of the exterior and interior

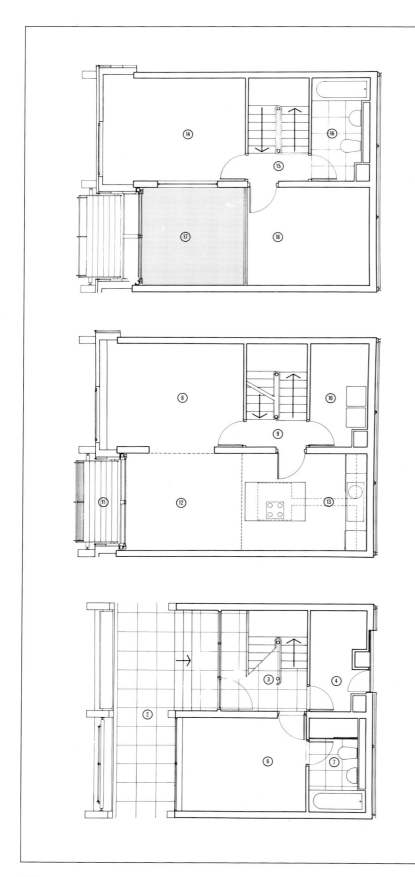

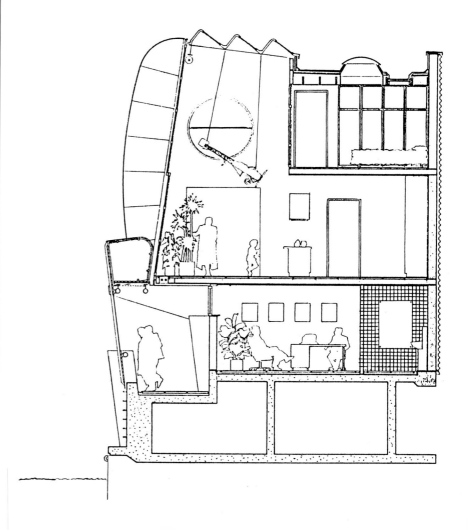

170

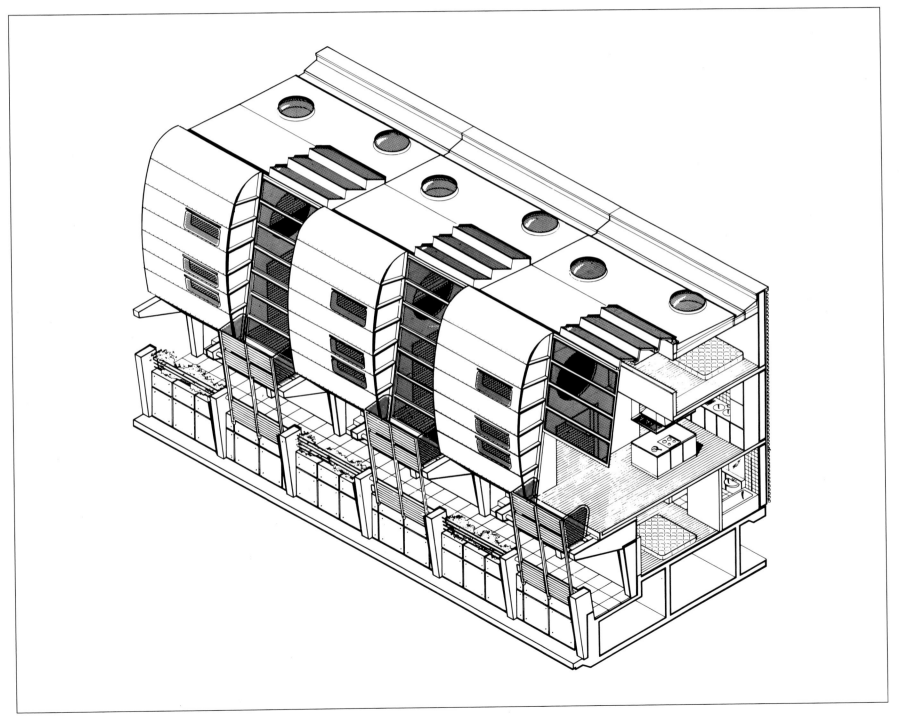

174

Architects: Wolf D. Prix, Helmut Swiczinsky, Coop Himmelblau

Collaborators: Frank Stepper, Fritz Mascher, Franz Sam

Apartment-Complex Vienna 2

Lasallestrasse

1983-1988   Vienna (A)

This complex, comprising large and small shop units, offices, studios and apartments, was designed for an empty plot on one of the avenues leading from the centre of Vienna to the outskirts.

The project created by the architects' cooperative founded by the Viennese Wolf D. Prix and Helmut Swiczinsky is based on the exploration of new spaces for residential units and the relationship which should hold between them, on the understanding that the city is a changing entity closely involved in the social problems of its inhabitants.
It was probably this premise which made it possible to break with what we would recognise as being architectural tradition and urban context. Thought out around the creation of a central public circulation core, its progression in three dimensions, together with dislocations and independent sequences, determined the configuration of the outer volume.

Although the building is a repository for highly personal conceptual strategies, it is easy to imagine how the act of coming home to one's apartment here would be a new experience, enlivened by events prompted by the spatial layout generated by the scheme.

The project formulates the basic rights of the resident: the right to live in a spacious and economical setting in which one can intervene freely, without worrying about when or how.
The architects define the complex as 'open architecture', free, without false significations. This is a solution to the housing problem in all three dimensions, in which self-expressive forms and interlinking spaces indicate the infinite number of possibilities and variations to be found in the interior.

The project consists of two oblique elements whose displacement produces inclined surfaces, between which two volumes in the form of a flame emerge, where fifty apartments are laid out for the residents themselves to complete through their choice of finish for the interiors. All of the apartments have different dimensions, surfaces and

distributions, but all are laid out over two levels, which together have an average height of six metres, with a surface area of at least two hundred square metres.

There is also a built space of approximately 1,000 square metres for the free use of the residents, and premises on the ground floor set aside for offices, stores and workshops. The building's various different volumes and wings communicate by means of a neural system of lifts, stairs and a ramp which rises diagonally from one end of the block to the other.

The vitality of movement and the fantasy, along with the study of the space to be constructed, are the essential characteristics of this scheme, represented by the intuitive fashion in which the first sketches were instantly transformed into working models. Lines were rapidly converted into forms, which in turn made way for a structure that is highly complex and precise at the same time.

This need for the arbitrary, very different from the need for function, is what leads the project to a chaotic, disorganised continent. The structure, its form and the interior thus created derive from initial design ideas in which imagination and invention collaborate to give rise to a 'nervous architecture' of inexplicable elements.

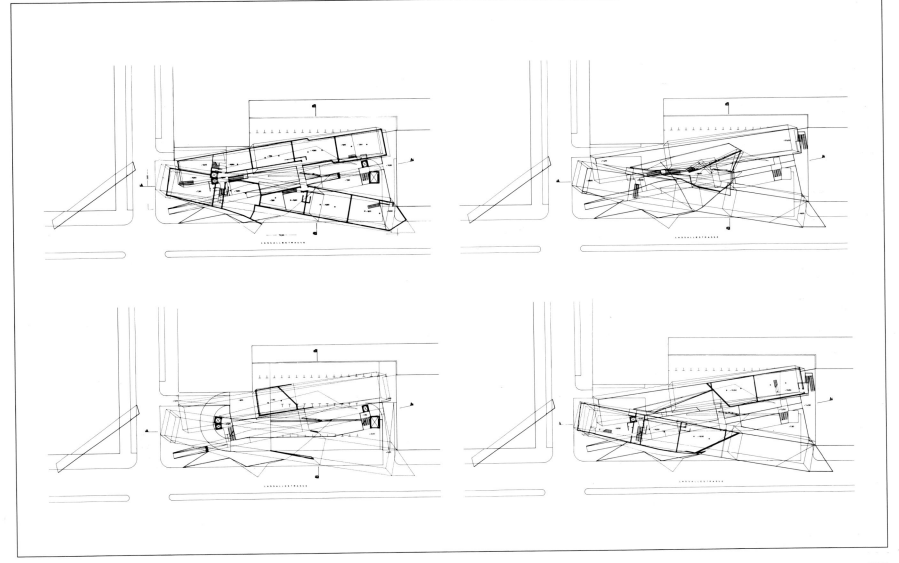

Architect: Steven Holl

Collaborators: Lorcan O'Herlihy, Peter Lynch, Peter Shinoda, Darius Sollohub, Stephen Cassell

Hybrid Building

1985-1988   Seaside, Florida (US)

Seaside is a new city, currently under construction, by the shores of the Gulf of Mexico on the coast of the state of Florida. The urban design and planning criteria have established, in the interests of a uniform image, tight restrictions with respect to height, typologies, and the basics of design and services to be incorporated into the buildings. Accordingly, this project was to form part of a continuous arcade running around a public square.

Occupying a relatively small plot of land, this is the first building to be constructed in Seaside, the aim of which is to create a prototype for the subsequent urban development.
The Hybrid Building combines various different uses, with shopping on the ground floor, offices on the first floor, and dwellings above. the concentration of these different programmes creates an incidental urbanism, intensifying the idea of a hybrid building for a 'society of strangers', as the architect describes it.

"...The building is divided in its upper levels into two volumes differentiated by their orientation. The west-facing block, receiving light from the setting sun, with its facade looking onto the central square, is intended for sociable types who get up late and like action through to the small hours. All of the apartments have two levels, and are identical. They are fitted with luxury bathrooms, microwave ovens and party areas.
The east-looking apartments, oriented towards the rising sun and the dawn, are intended for melancholy individuals. These like to wake early, to enjoy silence and solitude. The melancholy types for whom these dwellings were conceived are: a tragic poet, a musician and a mathematician. For this reason the floor plans and sections of the three apartment types are developed along the same lines.

The tragic poet's home is bathed in a tenuous light, sifted by identical windows, very tall and narrow. The canopy of the roof attempts to reproduce the effect of a farmhouse tablecloth.
In the musician's house, the light spills into the room from the windows on the upper level. A wall rendered in black plaster smoothly

ascends from the ground floor to the roof, emphasising the fluidity of space in movement.

In the mathematician's home everything is imperceptibly distorted. The stairs going up to the second level change their natural state over the bathroom. The change in direction of the wooden purlins which support the roof forms a gently warped surface. On the second level is the table for carrying out calculations, with a shelf on which lies a skull, in homage to the celebrated Johannes Kepler and the skull that always presided over his desk. ..."

The accesses to each block are independent, but a lift which seems not to want to form part of the building's design owes its peripheral location to the apparently unimportant relationship with the spaces which it serves. There is a courtyard between the two residential blocks, thought of as a meeting place for the people who live there.

The painstaking effort in the creation of the proportions - based on the golden mean to determine the dimensions of the windows, arches and walls - or the interiors of each apartment, configured by the intrinsic textures of the materials used, all contribute to the subtle development of this project. The building's construction is based on rapidly assembled prefabricated systems in the form of concrete columns, pillars, beams and perforated panels; The walls formed of concrete blocks are rendered with grey-tinted plaster.

The Hybrid Building starts out from an anecdotal programme, the construction of a simple block of apartments in front of a square, and then goes on to develop an architectonic conception that is imaginative and highly individualised in terms of the premises of its occupants.

Section, axonometric drawing of the project
as a whole, plans and perspective

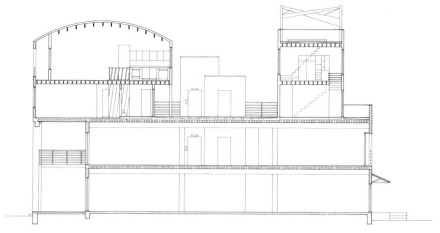

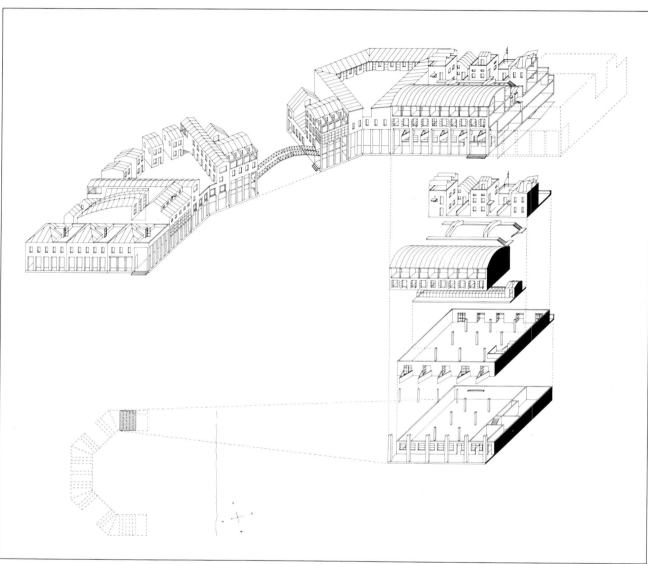

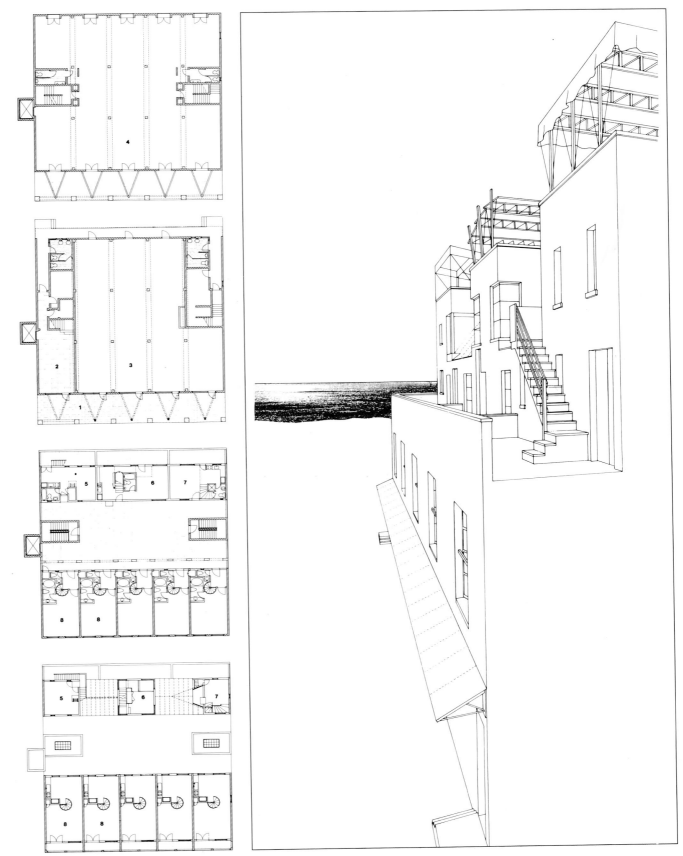

Various views of the exterior and interior

Bibliography

General bibliography

AAVV, *Housing in Europa, prima parte 1900-1960,* Edizioni Luigi Parma, Bologna, 1978

Hannah Arendt, *The human condition,* The University of Chicago Press, Chicago, 1958

Carlo Aymonino, *La vivienda racional. Ponencias de los Congresos del CIAM 1929-1930,* Editorial Gustavo Gili, S. A., Barcelona, 1973

Carlo Aymonino, *Orígines y desarollo de la ciudad moderna,* Colección Ciencia Urbanística, Editorial Gustavo Gili, S. A., Barcelona, 1972

Leonardo Benevolo, *Diseño de la ciudad-5. El arte y la ciudad contemporánea,* Editorial Gustavo Gili, S. A., Barcelona, 1977

W. Boesiger, *Le Corbusier. Oeuvre Complete,* Gisberger, Zurich, 1972

Giorgio Ciucci/Maristella Casciato, *Franco Marescotti e la casa civile 1934-1956,* 4. Architettura/Progetto, Officina Edizioni, Rome, 1980

Ulrich Conrads, *Barcelona, 1973*

Cesar Díaz/Pere Joan Ravetllat, *Habitatge i tipus a l'arquitectura catalana,* Edicions C.O.A. Catalunya, Barcelona, 1989

I. Diottalevi/Franco Marescotti, *Ordine e destino delle Case Popolare,* Domus, Milan, 1941

Kenneth Frampton, *Historia crítica de la arquitectura moderna,* Editorial Gustavo Gili, S. A.. Barcelona, 1981

Kenneth Frampton, *Modern architecture and the critical present,* Architectural Design Profile, Architectural Design and Academy Editions, London, 1982

G.A.T.E.P.A.C., *A.C./G.A.T.E.P.A.C. 1931-37,* Editorial Gustavo Gili, S. A., Barcelona, 1975

Giorgio Grassi, *Das Neue Frankfurt,* E. Dedalo, Bari, 1975

E. A. Griffini, *Construzione razionale della casa,* Hoepli, Milan, 1946

N. I. Habraken, *El diseño de soportes,* Editorial Gustavo Gili, S. A., Barcelona, 1979

Ludwig Hilberseimer, *La arquitectura de la gran ciudad,* Editorial Gustavo Gili, S. A., Barcelona, 1979

Le Corbusier/Pierre Jeanneret, *Oeuvres completes,* 8 vol., Les editions d'architecture, Zurich, 1971

Christian Norberg-Schulz, *L'abitare, l'insediamento, lo spazio urbano, la casa,* Electa Deitrice, Milan, 1984

Paul Ricoeur, *La metáfora viva,* Ediciones Megalopolis, Asociación Editorial La Aurora, Buenos Aires, 1977

Roger Sherwood, *Vivienda: Prototipos del Movimiento Moderno,* Editorial Gustavo Gili, S. A., Barcelona, 1983

Raymond Unwin, *La practica della progettazione urbana,* Collezione Struttura e Forma Urbana, Il Saggiatore, Milan, 1971

Bibliography of Works and Projects

Ponto e Vírgula. The Hague

Alvaro Siza: 1954-1988, A+U, Tokyo, 1989
Alexandre Alves Costa/Wilfried Wang, Alvaro Siza: figures and configurations, buildings and projects 1986-1988, Rizzoli, New York, 1988

Alvaro Siza: profesión poética, Editorial Gustavo Gili, S. A., Barcelona, 1988

Magazines: Arq 88/nº 271-272; AV 89/nº 19; Cas 87/nº 538; Domus 89/nº 705; AA 89/nº 261; Q 88/nº 178.

Max-Planck-Strasse. Erding, Munich

Magazines: A+U 82/nº 145; AA 82/nº 222; Q 88/nº 178; T&A 83/nº 347.

Kop St. Janshaven. Rotterdam

Magazine: T&A 89/nº 383.

Hillekop. Rotterdam

Magazines: AA 89/nº 266; AV 89/nº 19; T&A 89/nº 383.

Block 10 IBA. Berlin

Alberto Ferlenga, *Aldo Rossi,* Electa Editrice, Milan, 1990
Peter Arnell/Ted Bickford (eds.), *Aldo Rossi: obras y proyectos,* Editorial Gustavo Gili, S. A., Barcelona, 1986
Gianni Braghieri, *Aldo Rossi,* Editorial Gustavo Gili, S. A., Barcelona, 1991

Magazines: AVi 90/nº 14; AV 86/nº 7; Bau 89/nº 4; Domus 88/nº 697; AA 89/nº 263; Lotus 88/nº 57.

Polígono Los Corrales. Cadiz

Magazine: Croquis 86/nº 26.

Nemausus 1. Nîmes

Patrice Goulet, *Jean Nouvel,* Electa Moniteur, Paris, 1987
Jean Nouvel: l'obra recent, 1987-1990, COAC-Quaderns monografies, Barcelona, 1990

Magazines: AMC 88/nº 19; A Rec 88/nº 6; AC 88; AI 85/nº 209; A+U 88/nº 214; Bau 89/nº 4; Baw 87/n'42; Blu 88/nº 50; CV 89/nº 211; L'Ar 88/nº 16; AA 87/nº 252 - 88/nº 260; L'A 88/nº 391; Q 89/nº 181-182; SD 89/nº 299; T&A 87/nº 375; WBW 90/nº 3.

The Imperial. Miami, Florida

Magazines: AA 84/nº 235; Blu 86/nº 30; Domus 83/nº 641; GA 83/nº 7; PA 80/nº 1 - 82/nº 2; Q 90/nº 185; SD 84/nº 242.

City Edge IBA. Berlin

Philip Johnson/Mark Wigley, *Arquitectura Deconstructivista,* Editorial Gustavo Gili, S. A., Barcelona, 1988

Magazines: AA files 87/nº 14; AD 89/nº 12; Arq 88/nº 270; A+U 88/nº 215; Domus 88/nº 696.

Housing and Office Complex, Basle

Wilfried Wang, *Emerging European Architects,* Rizzoli, New York, 1988
Klassizismen und Klassiker, Katalog der Ausstellung des Badischen Kunstvereins, Hrsg. Frank Werner, Karlsruhe, March 23, 1985

Magazines: Abit 85/nº 240; Arch 86/nº 1; Cas 87/nº 535; Q 89/nº 183; WBW 83/nº 12 - 85/nº 4 - 85/nº 11 - 87/nº 1-2.

Block 1 IBA, Berlin

Magazines: Cas 85/nº 509; Dai 90/nº 35.

Single-Person Flats, Haringey, London

Kenneth Frampton, *Colquhoun, Miller and Partners,* Rizzoli, New York, 1988

Magazines: AJ 81/nº 9; A Rev 83/nº 1034; Arq 83/nº 240; A+U 82/nº 139; Bau 82/nº 11 - 84/nº 4; Cas 89/nº 562; OP 84/nº 26; Biba London Region Year Book 81; T&A 83/nº 351.

Hutweidenhof, Berlin-Tegel

Gustav Peichl, Massimo Scolari, Editorial Gustavo Gili, S. A., Barcelona, 1987

Magazines: AV 88/nº 15; AA 84/nº 235; T&A 84/nº 356.

Plaça d'Espanya, Sabadell, Barcelona

Cesar Díaz/Pere Joan Ravetllat, *Habitatge i tipus a l'arquitectura catalana,* Publicacions del Col.legi d'Arquitectes de Catalunya, Barcelona, 1989

Magazines: AV 87/nº 11; Q 85/nº 164; T&A 87/nº 371.

Avinguda Icària, Barcelona

Magazine: Arq 89/nº 278-279.

Catex Poble Nou, Barcelona

Magazines: Arq 89/nº 278-279; Cas 87/nº 535; Croquis 90/nº 42; AA 89/nº 246; On 89/nº 103.

Luisenplatz, Berlin

Wilfried Wang, *Emerging European Architects,* Rizzoli, New York, 1988
Hans Kollhoff, introduction by Fritz Neumeyer, Editorial Gustavo Gili, S. A., Barcelona, 1991

Magazines: AJ 89/nº 6; A Rev 87/nº 1082; Arq 89/nº 278-279; Q 88/nº 176; AV 85/nº 2 - 87/nº 7; Cas 86/nº 522; Domus 88/nº 697; T&A 89/nº 383.

Schwarz Park, Basle

Herzog & de Meuron, introduction by Josep Lluís Mateo, Editorial Gustavo Gili, S. A., Barcelona, 1989

Magazines: A3 nº 10; AMC 88/XII; Cas 88/IX; Forum nº 1; Q 87/nº 175 - nº 181 - nº 182 - nº 183.

Piazza a San Pietro a Patierno, Naples

Francesco Venezia, introduction by Alvaro Siza Vieira, Editorial Gustavo Gili, S. A., Barcelona, 1988

Magazines: Arq 89/nº 278-279 - 89/nº 281; Modo 89/nº 111; Q 87/nº 175.

Polígono 38, La Paz, Madrid

Xavier Güell (ed.), *Arquitectura española contemporánea. La década de los 80,* introduction by Joseph Rykwert, Editorial Gustavo Gili, S. A., Barcelona, 1990

Magazines: AD 88/III; AV 86/nº 5; D'A 89/nº 3; Croquis 88/nº 32-33; AA 91/nº 273; On 88/nº 89.

Cloudy-Spoon. Hoya, Tokyo

Magazines: AD 88/nº 5-6; A Rec 88/nº 2; GA 90/nº 25; JA 86/næ 355-356 - 87/nº 360 - 89/nº 385.

Asunto-Oy Hiiralankaari

An Architectural present: 7 approaches, Museum of Finnish Architecture, 1990
Gullichsen/Kairama/Vormala, introduction by Colin St John Wilson, Editorial Gustavo Gili, S. A., Barcelona, 1990

Magazines: Ark 83/nº 8; A+U 88/nº 209; Bau 85/nº 5; Cas 90/nº 573; T&A 84/nº 356.

Cube II-III. Amagasaki, Hyogo

Like a master watchmaker, SUMAI Library Publishing Company, Tokyo, 1990
Yukio Futagawa/Riichi Miyake, *Shin Takamatsu,* G.A. Architect 9, A.D.A. Edita, Tokyo, 1990
Xavier Guillot, *Shin Takamatsu: architectural works: 1981-1989,* Electa Moniteur, Paris, 1989
The Killing Moon, Folio XII, Architectural Association, London, 1988

Magazine: Blu 89/nº 61.

Grand Union Walk, London

Nicholas Grimshaw & Partners, Book 1 Product, Book 2 Process, NGP, London, 1988

Magazines: AJ 86/VIII - 89/nº 14; BD 86/VIII; AA 90/nº 267; L'Arch 90/nº 415; A Rec 89/nº 9; A Rev 89/nº 112; Royal Fine Art Commission: Annual Report 1986.

Apartment-Complex Vienna 2, Vienna

Philip Johnson/Mark Wigley, *Arquitectura Deconstructivista,* Editorial Gustavo Gili, S. A., Barcelona, 1988
Michael Sorkin, *Folio XIII Coop Himmelblau: Blaubox,* AA Publications, London, 1988

Magazines: AA files 85/nº 9 - 90/nº 19; A+U 89/nº 226; AV 88/nº 15; Blu 89/nº 53; Croquis 89/nº 40; AA 85/nº 239; T&A 85/nº 358.

Hybrid Building, Seaside, Florida

Steven Holl, *Anchoring,* Princeton Architectural Press, New York, 1989
Stuart Wrede, *Emilio Ambasz/Steven Holl: Architecture,* The Museum of Modern Art exhibition catalogue, New York, 1989
The emerging generation in USA: Steven Holl, G.A. Houses, Special 2, Tokyo, 1987

Magazines: AA files nº 14; A+U 88/1; Lotus 96/nº 50; PA 87/I - 88/XII - 89/VIII.

Magazine abbreviations

A3	A3 Times (GB)	Blu	Blueprint (GB)
AA	L'Architecture d'Auourd'hui (F)	Cas	Casabella (I)
AA files	AA files (GB)	Croquis	El Croquis (E)
Abit	Abitare (I)	CV	Casa Vogue (I)
AC	Architecture Contemporaine (F)	Dai	Daidalos (GB)
AD	Architectural Design (GB)	Domus	Domus (I)
AI	Architecture Interieure CREE (F)	Forum	Forum (NL)
AJ	The Architects' Journal (GB)	GA	Global Architecture Document (J)
AMC	Architecture Mouvement Continuité (F)	JA	The Japan Architect (J)
A Rec	Architectural Record (USA)	L'A	L'Architettura (I)
A Rev	The Architectural Review (GB)	L'Ar	L'Arca (I)
Arch	Architese (CH)	Lotus	Lotus International (I)
Ark	Arkkitehti (SF)	Modo	Modo (I)
Arq	Arquitectura (E)	On	On (E)
A+U	Architecture + Urbanism (J)	Op	Oppositions (USA)
AV	A&V, Monografias de Arquitectura y Vivienda (E)	PA	Progressive Architecture (USA)
AVi	Arquitectura Viva (E)	Q	Quaderns (E)
Bau	Baumeister (D)	SD	Space Design (J)
Baw	Bauwelt (CH)	T&A	Techniques & Architecture (F)
BD	Building Design (GB)	WBW	Werk, Bauen + Wohnen (D)

Photographers

Ponto e Virgula
José Rodrigues - Atelier 18

Max-Plank-Strasse
Wolfgang Gröschel

Kop St. Janshaven
Hectic Pictures
Hans Werlemanp
Daria Scagliola

Hillekop
Houben
Bastian Ingenhousz

Block 10 IBA
Uwe Rau

Polígono Los Corrales
Duccio Malagamba

Nemausus 1
Deidi von Schaeven

The Imperial
Norman McGrath

City Edge IBA
Uwe Rau

Housing & Office Complex

Block 1 IBA
Dieter Leistner

Single-Person Flats
Martin Charles

Hutweidenhof
Van der Vlugt & Klaus

Plaça d'Espanya
Luís Casals

Avinguda Icària
Foto CB

Catex Poble Nou
Martí Gasull
Pau Giralt
Manolo Laguillo
Ferran Freixa

Luisenplatz
Uwe Rau

Schwarz Park

Piazza a San Pietro a Patierno

Polígono 38, La Paz
Javier Azurmendi

Cloudy-Spoon
Kenichi Suzuki (Shinkenchiku)

Asunto-Oy Hiiralankaari
Simo Rista

Cube II-III
Toshiyuki Kobayashi/Retoria

Grand Union Walk
Jo Reid & John Peck

Apartment-Complex Vienna 2
Gerald Zugmann

Hybrid Building
Paul Warchol/Wayne Fujii

Acknowledgements

My thanks to the architects of the projects which appear on these pages for their invaluable cooperation in making it possible to illustrate this book, and my indebtedness to the efficient coordination of the publishing staff at Gustavo Gili, and in particular to Elena Llobera. I would also like to express my appreciation of Ignasi Pérez's laborious work of advance documentation, which significantly facilitated the final result. Finally, and especially, I must declare my gratitude to Gustavo Gili and Xavier Güell, who undoubtedly contributed to extending the scope of this book.

Pere Joan Ravetllat Mira